dali

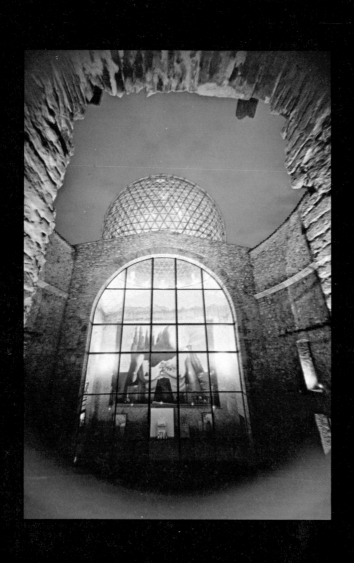

dali

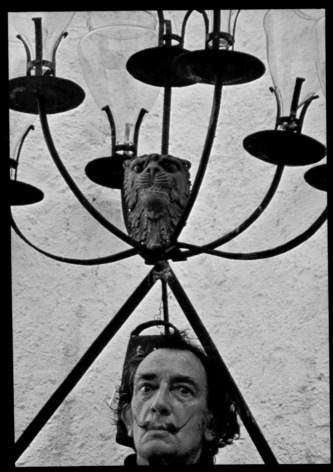

conroy maddox

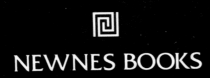

NEWNES BOOKS

The author and publishers would like to thank Salvador Dali and Enrique Sabater for their kind co-operation in preparing this book.

Title spread left: The Dali Museum, at Figueras, Spain.

Published by Newnes Books
a division of
The Hamlyn Publishing Group Limited
84/88 The Centre, Feltham, Middlesex, TW13 4BH

© The Hamlyn Publishing Group Limited 1979, Newnes Books 1983

First published 1979
Softback edition published 1981
Second impression 1983

ISBN 0 600 34263 8

Printed and bound in Spain
by Graficromo, S.A. — Cordoba

contents

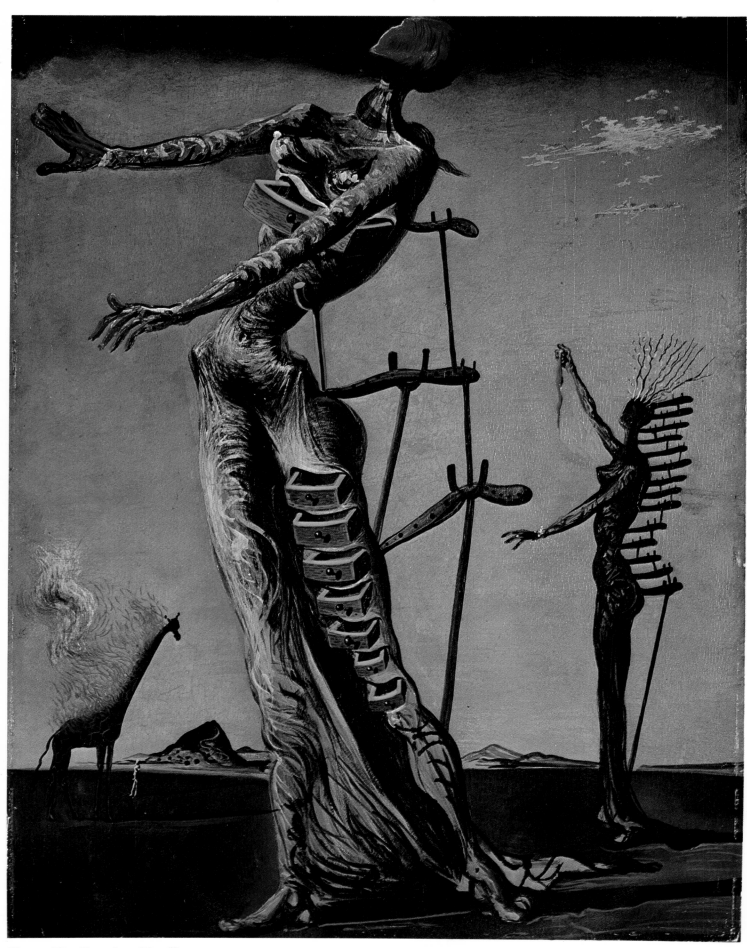

Plate 1 **The Burning Giraffe**

6

introduction

Whatever the future judgement of Salvador Dali may be, it cannot be denied that he has a place all his own in the history of modern art. His fame has been an issue of controversy, kept alive as much by Dali's own provocative exhibitionism as by the critics and press, who have so consistently condemned him for his excesses: 'neurotic', 'egocentric' and 'mad' are words not infrequently used when referring to him. Over the years he has become so closely identified with Surrealism that it is possible to say that in the public mind Surrealism simply is Salvador Dali. Considering the publicity there is some excuse for this prevailing error.

Whatever his influence has been on the art of the 20th century, few can deny the validity of his contribution. In fact, it could be argued that it is as great as that of his famous fellow-countryman, Picasso. Dali himself has said: 'Picasso is less of a painter, but he is the most destructive genius of modern times.' Certainly the revelatory nature of Dali's imagery between 1929 and 1939 was the most potent of our age, which makes it that much more difficult to assess its aesthetic worth. From early childhood he was abnormally imaginative, selfishly preoccupied with his own pleasures, cynically parading his audacity and his perverse violence, the intimate details of which he did not hesitate to boast of in his memoirs. In his book *Surrealism* Julien Levy sees him as 'a man who bears the stigma of the Spanish Inquisition, the sexual ecstasies of Spain's mystics . . .' and we have only to explore the iconography of his work to affirm the connection with that Spanish heritage.

If the problem is correctly stated, then Dali, though not alone in the field (the Surrealist Manifesto was launched in 1924, some five years before Dali's involvement), is perhaps the first to have consistently exploited the findings of Freud and psychoanalysis and to have deliberately insisted on the rights of man to his own madness. His development of a 'paranoiac-critical' approach, which he brought, to bear so excessively into all aspects of thought, was one of the most revolutionary contributions to Surrealism and was the touchstone which gave Dali's work its unique character and dominated his evolution as an artist. To follow his development is to follow the

Plate 1
The Burning Giraffe
1935
Oil on canvas
$10\frac{5}{8} \times 13\frac{3}{4}$ in (27 × 35 cm)
Kunstmuseum, Basel

By 1934, Dali's use of what he called 'handmade photography', with its sharply defined colour areas, had given way to a more aesthetic use of colour as well as a lyricism in his handling of form.

Plate 2
Beach Scene with Telephone
1938
Oil on canvas
29 × 36¼ in (73 × 92 cm)
Edward James Foundation

Dali's interest in the telephone dates from the Munich crisis of 1938 that preceded the Second World War.

fertile imagination and manual dexterity that he was to bring to Surrealism at a particular time. As early as 1920 André Breton, who was to play such an important part in the Surrealist movement, had proposed 'allegiance to folly, to dreams, to the incoherent, to the hyperbolic – in a word to all that is contrary to the general appearance of reality'. Several years would go by before Dali was to make his pictorial and critical participation; it is necessary, therefore, that we trace his development and the influences that were to have such a crucial effect on what he was to call his images of 'concrete irrationality'.

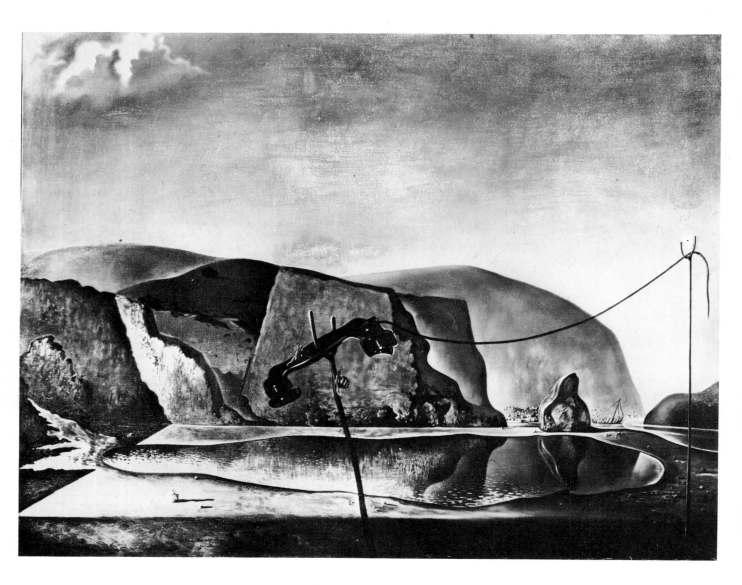

biography

Salvador Dali was born at eight forty-five on the morning of 11th May 1904, in the Spanish town of Figueras, where his father was a notary and man of some local importance. The name Salvador had originally been given to his brother who had died three years before Dali was born. An only child until his sister Ana María arrived, he was thoroughly spoilt and allowed to do almost anything he pleased. In his autobiography, Dali gives a vivid account of these early years: 'My brother and I resembled each other like two drops of water, but we had different reflections. Like myself he had the unmistakeable facial morphology of a genius. He gave signs of alarming precocity, but his glance was veiled by a melancholy, characterising insurmountable intelligence. I, on the other hand, was much less intelligent but I reflected everything. I was to become the prototype *par excellence* of the phenomenally retarded "polymorphous perverse" having kept intact all the reminiscences of the nursling's erogenic paradises; I clutched at pleasure with boundless, selfish eagerness and on the slightest provocation I would become dangerous.'[1] He does not neglect to record other memories, such as his intra-uterine life 'as though it were yesterday'; he identifies it as paradise, and also the colour of hell, but soft, warm and immobile. One of his pre-birth visions, he tells us, was that of a pair of eggs fried in a pan—but without the pan—'an ever-hallucinatory image' which he could later reproduce at will, a phosphene.[2]

His education began in a local school and then in the Academy in Figueras, run by the Brothers of the Marist Order. It was a period of little learning, and his school reports were received by his parents with consternation. A desire to do the exact opposite of what everyone else did assumed immense importance in his eyes, and hours were spent dreaming up the most anti-social acts in order to astonish his schoolmates. Many revealed themselves in acts of aggression. Walking with a young boy one day, he pushed him over a bridge on to the rocks some fifteen feet below, and then spent the afternoon eating cherries in a rocking chair as he watched the blood-stained basins being brought from the bedroom. Alone with his three-year-old sister, he dealt her a terrible kick on the head, which gave him a

[1]From *The Secret Life of Salvador Dali*, by Salvador Dali, translated by Haakon M. Chevalier, new enlarged edition 1961, copyright © 1946, 1961 by Salvador Dali, used with permission of the Dial Press. British and Commonwealth edition Vision Press, London.

[2]A sensation that results from pressure on the closed eyes.

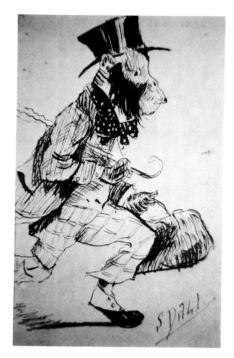

Plate 3
Satirical drawing
1920
Ink on cardboard
Collection Enrique Sabater

One of Dali's earliest known works, this cartoon was done as a present for his uncle.

'delirious joy'. He was given a wounded bat one day and took it to his hiding place in a wash-house. Next morning it lay, half dead, covered with frenzied ants. Overcome with emotion, he bit into the writhing mass. He also found an inexplicable pleasure in throwing himself down steps. The pain was insignificant, the intense joy was overwhelming, and he was encouraged to repeat the performance many times, not unaware of the effect it produced on his fellow pupils. On another occasion he smashed a boy's violin to prove that painting was superior to music.

Before Dali was six years old, he was showing considerable talent as an artist. Fleur Cowles in her book[1] on Dali reproduces the earliest known work, a landscape painted postcard-size. It was followed by two much more ambitious works, *Portrait of Helen of Troy* and *Joseph Greeting his Brethren*, executed in the precise 19th-century literary style. For a studio, Dali was given the use of an old wash-house at the top of the house. On hot days he would fill a tub full of water, remove his clothes and sit in it for hours, painting. Pinned to the walls around were his paintings, carried out on the covers of hat boxes taken from his aunt's millinery shop, as well as reproductions of the Renaissance masters torn from magazines. Here he found refuge, and the solitude that he always so desperately sought. To be alone became a mania, and all kinds of excuses were found which would permit him to rush upstairs to the laundry. Here he felt unique, living out his fantasies, playing at being a genius: 'if you play at genius, you become one.'

Still subject to heights of delirious egocentricity, his parents, not unaware of his growing artistic ability, sent him to a friend of theirs in the country. Ramón Pitchot was a rich connoisseur of art and a gifted painter in the Impressionist manner. It was a considerably talented family. Two sons were musicians, one of the daughters was an opera singer and another was married to a Spanish poet. Their estate was known as the Muli de la Torre (The Tower Mill). Dali's period with this family was to have an important influence on his life and illuminates many of the erotic fantasies that were to appear in later works.

Although the practical side of the mill had little interest, the tower produced a powerful effect on his imagination. It became a 'sacred spot', the very centre of his world. Each day he would have his meals in a room hung with the many Impressionist paintings of Ramón Pitchot. To the young Dali these 'visual cocktails' with their brilliant decorative unity were an endless fascination. It was not long before he was deeply committed to this new and exciting way of looking at nature. 'It represented,' he tells us, 'my first contact with an anti-academic and revolutionary aesthetic theory.'

Pitchot provided him with a large whitewashed room as a studio where, consumed by a creative fever, he explored the instantaneous luminosity that he found so tantalising in these new paintings. On one occasion, having used up all his canvas, he decided to utilise an old wooden door, somewhat worm-eaten, for a subject that had been

[1] *The Case of Salvador Dali.*

in his mind for some time, a still-life of a large bunch of cherries. They were to be painted in three colours only and applied directly from the tube. Setting up an immense pile of cherries as a model, he attacked the wooden surface. Soon he found that he was painting to the rhythm of the mill, each cherry being realised with three touches of colour – vermilion for the lighter side, carmine for the shade, white for the highlight. The whole effect, with the thick daubs of colour, assumed an astonishing realism. Completely engrossed in keeping up with the sound of the mill, he discovered that he had forgotten to add the stems. 'Suddenly, I had an idea. I took a handful of cherries and began to eat them. As soon as one of them was swallowed, I would glue the stem directly to my painting in the appropriate place.' The gluing on of cherry stems produced an unforeseen effect of startling 'finish'. To further reinforce the realism, he then proceeded to introduce real worms into the wormholes, which looked as though they belonged to the painted cherries. It must have been an impressive work. Pitchot, who turned up at that moment, was heard to mutter, 'That shows genius.'

His time at the Tower Mill fell into a ritual. Waking in the morning he went through an exhibitionist fantasy with the maid. At breakfast,

Plate 4
Cadaqués
1923
Oil on canvas
38 × 50 in (96.5 × 127 cm)
Private collection

Cadaqués is a small fishing village where Dali spent his summers while still a student.

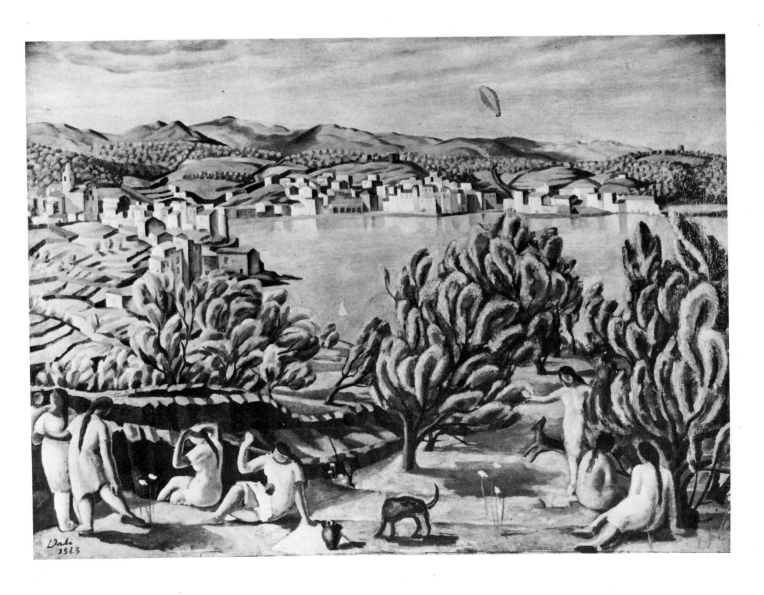

because he liked the sensation, he poured hot milk and coffee down his chest, then went to the studio to paint. Here, he tell us, he worked on 'pictorial inventions, re-invention of Impressionism, reaffirmation and rebirth of my aesthetic megalomania'.

Before Dali was to leave the Pitchots' there was a notable incident dominated by an object that was to find its way into his gallery of recurrent images. At the time of the linden blossom picking, helping to fetch the ladders from the tower attic, he discovered a heavy metal crown, used for some theatrical production, and an old crutch. It was an exciting find, loaded with fetishistic significance. Among the blossom pickers was an extremely attractive woman with large and turgescent breasts, accompanied by her twelve-year-old daughter. Dali instantly fell in love with the child, identifying her with all his false memories of the ideal woman. Finding his impulsive behaviour only succeeded in frightening the young girl, he found solace in

Plate 5
Apparatus and Hand
1927
Oil on panel
24½ × 18¾ in (62 × 47.5 cm)
Private collection

Between 1925 and 1928, Dali rejected his abstract experiments to come under the influence of Picasso and the Cubist movement. Nevertheless, he had not lost touch with his early training based on the realist tradition and continued to produce representational works of considerable technical precision. This work is beginning to show evidence of his growing hallucinatory power.

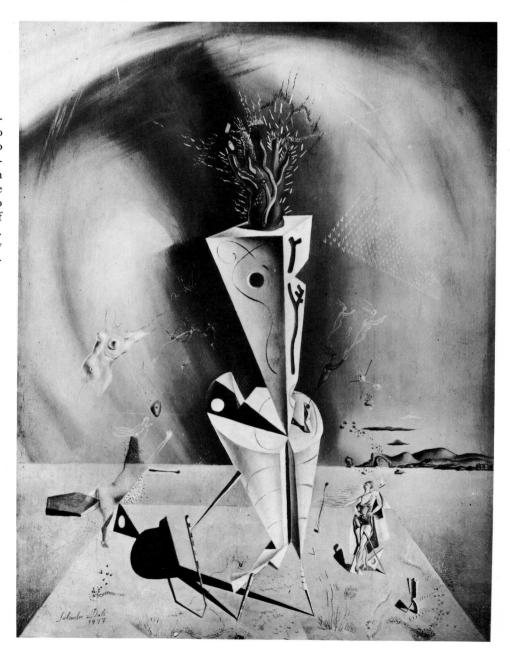

covertly watching the mother, in particular her large firm breasts, beneath which he had a voluptuous desire to rest the upper bifurcated part of the newly discovered crutch. Overcome with longing, he invented a ruse which could fulfil the fantasy. Finding a closed area lit only by a small window overlooking the garden, his attention was drawn to three melons hanging from the rafters. They suggested to his feverish mind a substitute even more desirable than the woman's breasts. Carefully entangling his diabolo in the vines that grew on the outside wall above the window, he then asked the blossom picker to retrieve the toy. While she moved the ladder to the desired spot, he rushed back to the room, stripped off his clothes, placed the crown on his head and covered himself with an ermine cloak. At the exact moment the upper part of the woman's body filled the small window space, he let slip the cloak from his naked body and gently placed the crutch beneath the lower part of one of the ripening melons, pressing it into the soft fruit, at the same time staring back and forth between the swollen breasts and the melon. Under the persistent pressure, the melon began to drip, covering him with its sweet and sticky juice. Further pressure detached the melon, which fell on to his head at the exact moment the woman, having disentangled the diabolo, descended the ladder. Hurriedly throwing himself on the floor he lay breathless, waiting, unsuccessfully, to be discovered. Trembling with exhaustion, the two remaining melons appeared as a 'sinister symbol and no longer evoked the beautiful blossom-gatherer's two breasts, sunny with afternoon. Instead, they too now seemed to stir like two dead things rolled into balls, like two petrified hedgehogs.'

The secret pleasure Dali derived from that crutch has remained with him ever since, not only as a fetish in erotic acts, but as a predominant image in many obsessive and fanciful ways in his paintings. Later he was to conceive the idea of a tiny facial crutch to be worn by 'criminally elegant women', so that they could experience 'the sacred tug of their exhibitionism encrusted in the flesh of their own faces'.

Encouraged by Pitchot, Dali's father enrolled him in Señor Nuñez's art classes in Figueras. Nuñez appears to have been a sympathetic teacher. Perhaps he sensed something of the later brilliance in his eccentric but dedicated pupil. Stimulated by the individual attention he received, Dali was soon reviving his passion for the great masters of the Renaissance and exploring the mysteries of chiaroscuro. Reading also began to be an obsession, with philosophy as his favourite subject. Nietzsche's *Thus Spake Zarathustra* and Voltaire's *Philosophical Dictionary* became firm favourites. His real joy was Kant, whom he read and re-read without understanding a word: 'such an important and useless book'. He dipped into Spinoza, and then Descartes on whom he was to base many of his later researches. His paintings were now beginning to attract attention, and invitations to show in local and regional exhibitions followed.

In the meanwhile, secondary studies continued at the Marist School, although most of the teachers had given up any hope of

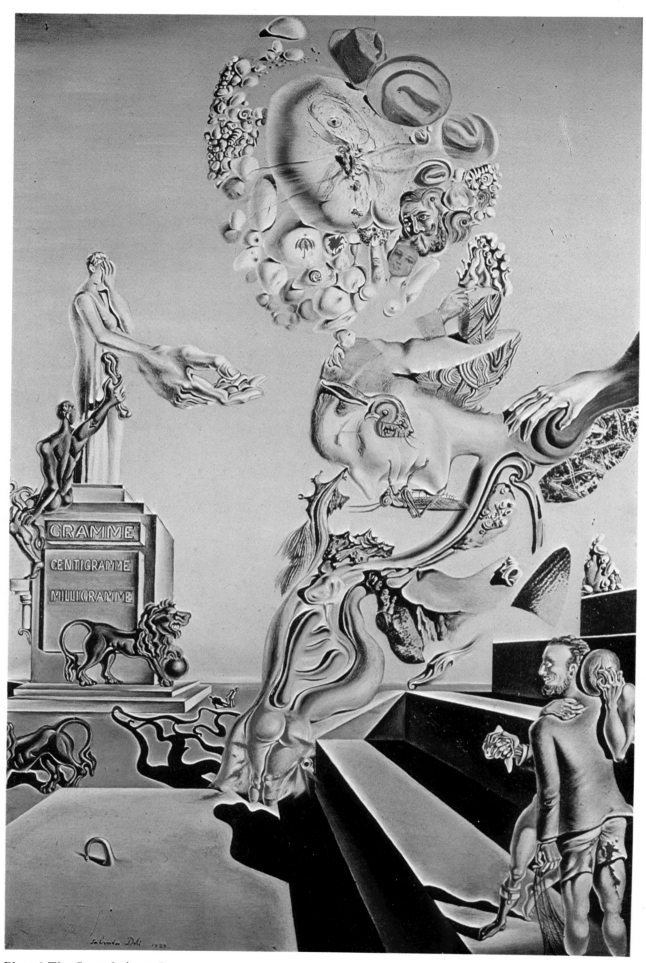

Plate 6 **The Lugubrious Game**

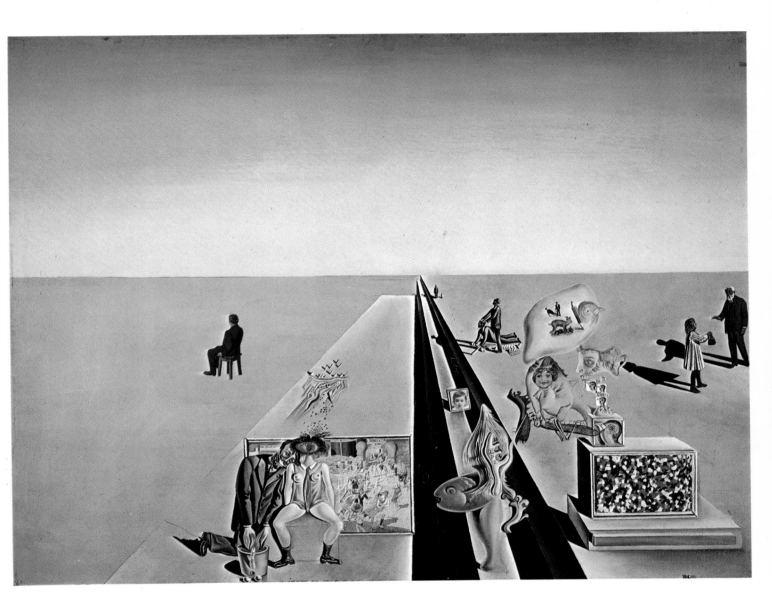

Plate 6
The Lugubrious Game
1929
Oil and collage on canvas
12¾ × 16⅛ in (31 × 41 cm)
Claude Hersaint Collection, Paris

The first truly Surrealist painting by Dali. The scatological elements were of some concern to the Surrealists when they first saw this work.

Plate 7
The First Days of Spring
1929
Oil on board with collage
19¾ × 25⅝ in (50 × 65 cm)
Private collection

Dali's working method during this period was to adapt the Surrealist processes of automatic writing to painting, of trying to see 'like a medium' the images that would appear in his imagination.

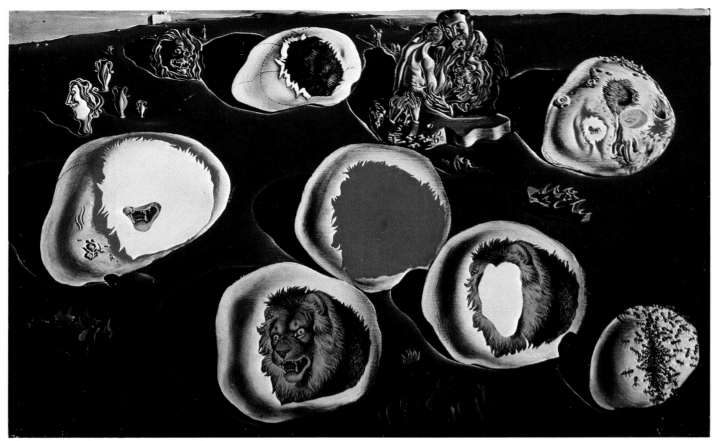

Plate 8 **Accommodations of Desire**

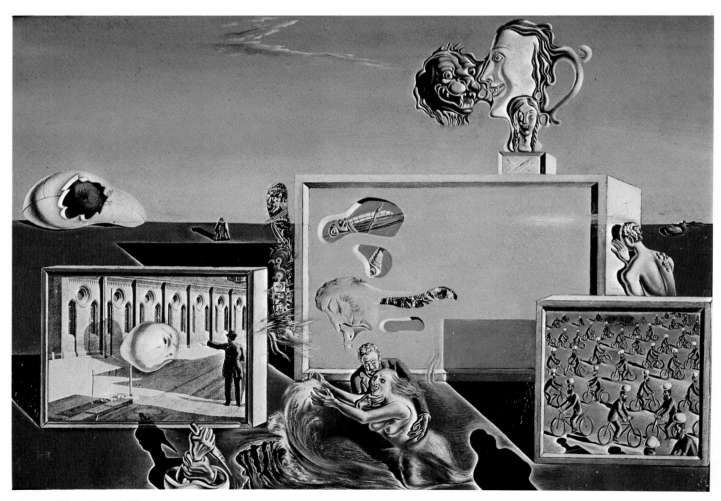

Plate 9 **Illumined Pleasures**

teaching him anything. Nose-bleeding and 'angina' became regular means of avoiding the hateful lessons. Frantically he awaited vacation time, which was always spent in the village of Cadaqués on the Mediterranean coast. The rocks and beaches which he came to know so well in his solitary wanderings became the very spot which he adored with a 'fanatical fidelity' and which he thought the most beautiful landscape in the world, with rocky contours that only Leonardo could have captured. It was to affect his vision profoundly: those strangely coloured rocks and deserted beaches are faithfully imprinted and appear in many studies with extraordinary love and clarity. Dali made the geological phenomena of Catalonia very much his own.

Although the family had little faith in his earning a living by art, they realised the futility of trying to convince their young son. A compromise was proposed, that he should attend the School of Fine Art in Madrid, qualify as a professor and use his free time to paint as he liked. Dali agreed with enthusiasm. He had been working hard and won two prizes. He was seventeen years of age and supremely confident of his ability. Suddenly Figueras was stifling, and Madrid offered independence, an escape from the watchful eyes of his family. Admission to the School of Fine Arts was dependent on an examination, a drawing of a classical subject made to exact measurements. According to Dali's account, he chose to ignore the instructions completely, making the drawing too small. Re-drawing, he made it too large. On the final day of submission, panic-stricken, he made another attempt, this time even smaller than the first. Nevertheless, so perfect was the study that he was accepted as a student.

For months he behaved as a model pupil. All social life was shunned. Sundays were spent at the Prado making Cubist sketches of the various paintings. He had just discovered one of the Cubist masters, Juan Gris, and was in full revolt against Impressionism. The rainbow palette was replaced with black, white, sienna and olive green. If the colours were sombre, the same could not be said of his attire. Long trousers were discarded in favour of short pants with stockings, sometimes puttees, a long waterproof cape, hair sticking out like a mane beneath a large black felt hat, and an unlit pipe clenched between his teeth. Whatever enthusiasm he had for the teaching ability at the Academy in the early months soon gave way to disappointment. He felt they had nothing to offer. To his searching questions about art, they had only evasive answers, such as: 'It's temperament that counts – no rules, no constraints. Simplify.' 'I was expecting to find limits, rigour, science,' he remarked, 'I was offered liberty, laziness, approximations.' Yet he continued to be an exemplary student, never missing a class and always respectful. The professors found him cold, too cerebral, but clever and always successful with his work.

His growing frustration with the Academy is amusingly highlighted by the incident of the plaster. One day, entering the sculpture room during the lunch period, he emptied sacks of plaster into a basin

Plate 8
Accommodations of Desire
1929
Oil on panel
$8\frac{5}{8} \times 13\frac{3}{4}$ in (22 × 35 cm)
Mr and Mrs Julien Levy
Collection, New York

Desire, for Dali, is expressed through the 'terrorising images of lions' heads'.

Plate 9
Illumined Pleasures
1929
Oil and collage on composition board
$9\frac{3}{8} \times 13\frac{3}{4}$ in (23.8 × 35 cm)
The Sidney and Harriet Janis Collection, Gift to the Museum of Modern Art, New York

Although part of this picture is composed of collage, the skilfully painted areas create confusion about what is paint and what is photography. Dali's debt to de Chirico is revealed in the picture within the picture as well as in the emotive use of perspective. Other influences derive from Max Ernst (the bird totem on the left of the centre box) and Magritte (the painted cyclists on the right). In a number of early works, he pasted down line engravings and photographs which were then faithfully copied so as to be indistinguishable from the original, as in another painting, *Accommodations of Desire* of 1929 (plate 8).

Plate 10
The Hand: Remorse
1930
Oil on canvas
$16\frac{1}{4} \times 26$ in (41.3 × 66 cm)
Private collection

The architecture and ornamentation of Art Nouveau with its 'undulant-convulsive' style is evident in this painting. The head of the girl behind the seated figure suggests that it was a direct copy from a work in the 'Modern Style'.

under the running tap. Soon the floor was inundated with the milk-white liquid which spread under the door and cascaded with catastrophic force down the stairway to spill out into the entrance hall. Thoroughly frightened by the magnitude of his action, he ploughed through the avalanche to the exit, but not before stopping to admire the fast-hardening mass.

It was about this time that he discovered Freud. *The Interpretation of Dreams* was of major importance in his life. The most casual act was subjected to agonising self-analysis, and he was to go through tortures trying to decide whether he was really mad. His dreams, he found, were always linked to an actual event, ending in the exact spot and the same situation in which he found himself upon awakening.

The artistic and literary developments in Europe, particularly Dadaism, with its mockery of all accepted values and sensational outbursts of exhibitionism, had not passed unnoticed among some of the students at the Academy. Luis Buñuel, García Lorca, Pedro Garfias and Eugenio Montes were the moving spirits of this small but wild band in which Dali was soon to occupy a position of importance. They praised his Cubist paintings, listened excitedly to his extravagant ideas. It was not long, he assures us, before it was 'Dali this, Dali that and Dali everything'. It was all very exciting. He became an habitué of the cafes, joining in the noisy intellectual discussions on art and literature, women and sex. The outlandish clothes were discarded for expensive suits and silk shirts, the pallid face was streaked with make-up, and he took to plastering his hair down with picture varnish.

An act of rebellion in support of one of the teachers brought about his temporary suspension from the Academy for a year. He returned to his worried father in Figueras, where shortly afterwards he was arrested by the Civil Guard and spent a month in prison. Considerable revolutionary agitation was taking place at the time, and Dali, with his wild talk of anarchy and monarchy, was immediately suspect. Since no charges could be found on which to try him, he was finally set free.

Again he left for Cadaqués, where he became an 'ascetic once more and where I literally gave myself over body and soul to painting and to my philosophic research'. He knew that once he returned to Madrid he would soon revert to the old ways. But in the meantime it was to be all discipline and work. 'I was in fact a monster,' he said, 'whose anatomical parts were an eye, a hand and a brain.'

At the end of the disciplinary period he returned to the Academy and immediately established his reputation for irreverence and rebellion. Given as a painting subject a Gothic statue of the Virgin, he chose to paint a pair of scales. 'Perhaps you see a virgin like everyone else,' he told the astonished teacher, 'I see a pair of scales.' There is little doubt that at this time Dali was going through several opposing experiments in painting. He explored the problems of Italian Futurism, particularly their attempts to suggest objects in motion. From 1924 the interest shifted to the Scuola Metafisica (the

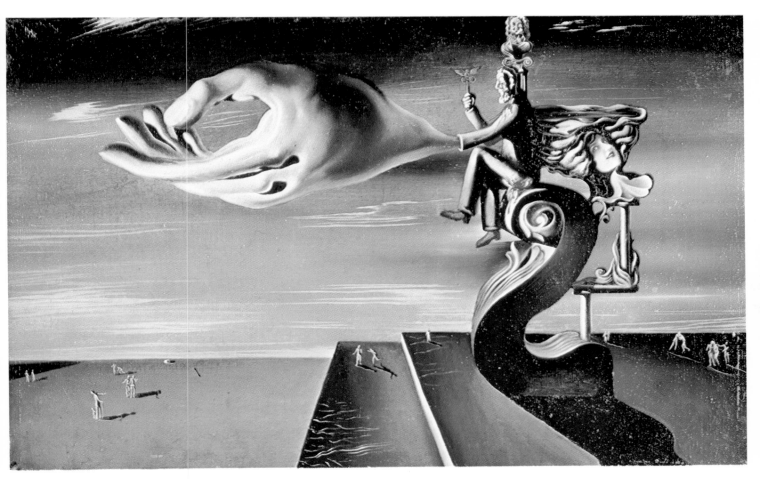

Plate 10 **The Hand: Remorse**

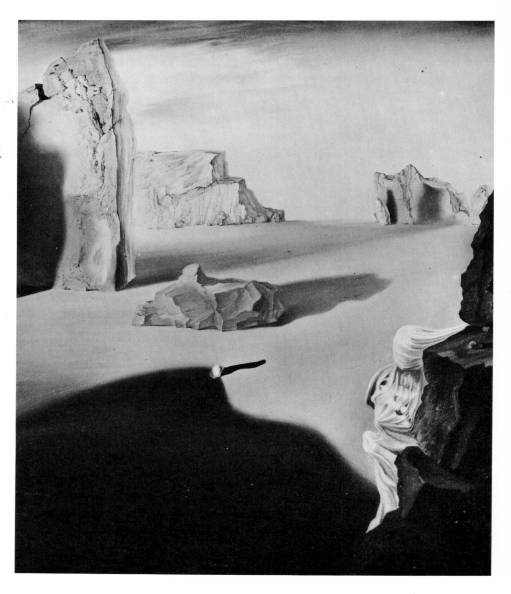

Metaphysical School), a movement evolved by Giorgio de Chirico and Carlo Carrà. De Chirico had had his art training in Munich, where he had come under the influence of the Swiss-German, Arnold Böcklin, with all his mysticism and romanticism. Nietzsche's writing on *Symbolical dream pictures* and Schopenhauer's *Essay on Apparitions* were to contribute to his enigmatic and disquieting dream imagery. The mystery of his city streets and deserted squares, with their own laws of perspective and veiled childhood memories, are some of the most poetic statements of our age. They proposed a rejection of Cubism and Futurism, affirming in their place an art of the metaphysical, a return to dreams and inner perception. In Paris the Surrealists had not failed to recognise the extreme originality of what de Chirico had achieved.

For Dali, it was to bring him that step nearer the means of externalising his obsessions. It was all the more surprising, therefore, in view of his later development in Surrealism and his vehement rejection of abstraction, that he should suddenly turn back to the Cubism of Picasso. James Thrall Soby puts forward the theory that 'Dali had inevitably to face the issue which Cubism had raised in European art. Reduced to a dramatic decision, this issue consisted in whether a given younger artist should be for or against Picasso's dictates', and he goes on to say: 'Remembering that Picasso was a fellow Catalan, one can understand why Dali should have been caught, at some point, by the immense suction of his ideas.' Yet it is not inconceivable that Dali sensed in the classical structure and abstracted subject-matter of Cubism a security that, at least for a time, would provide some steadying control over the disordered nature of his innermost thoughts, which were now beginning to possess him, thoughts that were no longer to lead a merely subjectively delusional existence, but were to be made objectively perceptible in painting. It is no accident that, after his rejection of Cubism, he should have painted *The Lugubrious Game* (plate 6), with its provocative scatology and in particular its coprophagic element.

Committing himself to Cubism, Dali undertook a visit to Paris in 1927 to see Picasso. According to Dali's account, he arrived deeply moved and full of respect. 'I have come to see you before visiting the Louvre,' he told the artist. 'You're quite right,' replied Picasso. Dali then showed him a small painting he had brought, which Picasso studied without comment. For the next two hours he contemplated the canvases that Picasso dragged from the studio, also without any comment. On his leaving, they exchanged glances which meant, Dali assures us, 'You get the idea?' 'I get it.'

Another account of this visit speaks of Dali taking a tape measure with him and in complete silence proceeding to measure the size of each canvas placed before him.

After his return to Figueras, Luis Buñuel proposed collaboration on a film which his mother was prepared to finance. Dali found the

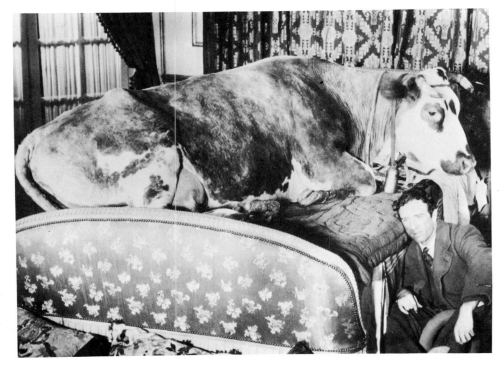

Plate 12
L'Age d'Or
The Golden Age
1931

After *Un Chien Andalou* in 1929, Dali and Buñuel collaborated on a second Surrealist film financed by the Vicomte de Noailles in 1931. Dali's scenario called for archbishops with embroidered tiaras bathing among the rocks of Cape Creus. He also suggested a few 'blasphematory scenes' which were to be presented with fanaticism in order to 'achieve the grandeur of a true and authentic sacrilege'.

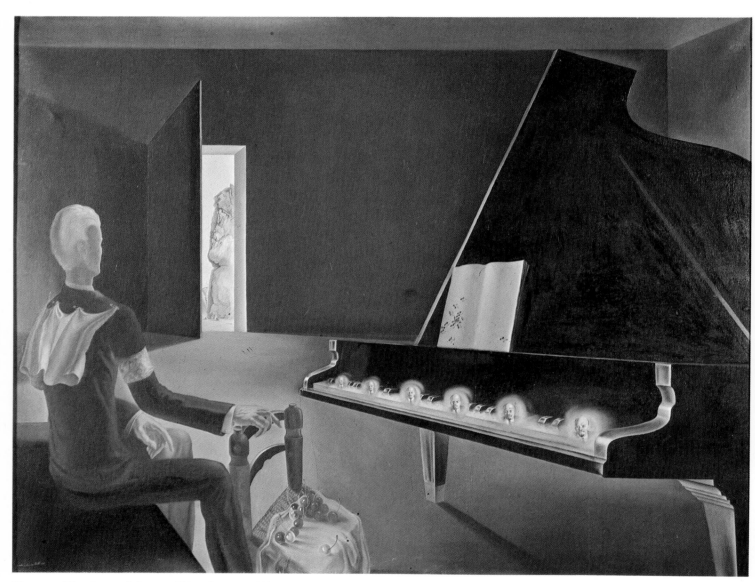

Plate 13 **Six Apparitions of Lenin on a Piano**

script naive and mediocre, and suggested in its place a scenario he had just completed. Its theme was of 'adolescence and death'. Together they worked on the plot, and also the title – it was to be called *Un Chien Andalou*. Buñuel hurried back to Paris to undertake the production, while Dali stayed behind to 'sharpen all my doctrinal means at a distance'.

His one-man exhibition at the Dalmau Gallery in Barcelona had been seen by Picasso during a brief visit to that city. Back in Paris he had spoken enthusiastically about the show to his dealer, Paul Rosenberg, who wrote asking for photographs, which Dali neglected to send. 'I knew,' he said, 'that the day I arrived in Paris, I would put them all in my bag with one sweep.' Another Spanish painter, Joan Miró, wrote and followed this up with a visit to Figueras with his gallery director, Pierre Loeb. For all Miró's generous support, Loeb remained sceptical, finding Dali's painting too confusing and lacking in personality. Dali must have found it a disappointment. Paris was where the battle was being fought and he intended, somehow, to participate in it. His exhibitions in Barcelona and Madrid had been highly successful, the reviews flattering. The magazine *d'Aci, d'Alla* had written: 'we are absolutely certain that if the young artist does not wander away, he will be one of those who will give the greatest glory to Catalan painting in our century ...' *La Publicidad* could not find among the young painters a more fascinating figure than that of this young man from Figueras. With the attention he was also getting from Paris, the very centre of the art world, his father was finally convinced that he should go.

The year was 1928 when Dali arrived in Paris. He was not thinking of another visit to Picasso, but, as he tells us, he turned to the taxi driver and asked, 'Do you know any good whorehouses?' 'Get in, Monsieur,' he answered, with somewhat wounded pride, though in a fatherly way. 'Don't worry, I know them all.'

He visited the 'Chabanais' which must have impressed him, for some twelve years later, speaking of the three spots that produced in him the deepest sense of mystery, he cited the stairway of the 'Chabanais' for its ugly eroticism, the Theatre of Palladio in Vicenza, the divine aesthetic, and the entrance to the tombs of the Kings of the Escorial as the 'most mysterious and beautiful mortuary spot'.

Miró did not desert his young friend and was full of advice on how to go about making the right connections in Paris society. First, he must get a dinner-jacket. He must not talk too much and go in for some physical culture. Tomorrow he would meet Tristan Tzara, the Dadaist leader. The social rounds continued – the Duchesse de Dato, the Comtesse Cuevas de Vera, Goemans, who was to become his dealer, Pavlik Tchelitchev, Robert Desnos, who wanted to buy his painting *The First Days of Spring* (plate 7). Pierre Loeb, who still hoped one day to show him, took him to the Bal Tabarin, where he met that 'legendary being,' Paul Eluard, the Surrealist poet. He looked in on Buñuel. *Un Chien Andalou* was going into production, and he helped with some of the effects. The requirements were

Plate 13
Six Apparitions of Lenin on a Piano
1931 or 1933
Oil on canvas
$57\frac{3}{8} \times 44\frac{7}{8}$ in (146 × 114 cm)
Musée National d'Art Moderne, Paris

Although Dali refused to associate himself with the revolutionary aspects of Surrealism, this painting was inspired by the leader of the Russian revolution. A less charitable portrayal of Lenin is to be seen in the painting *The Enigma of William Tell* (plate 23) painted in 1934.

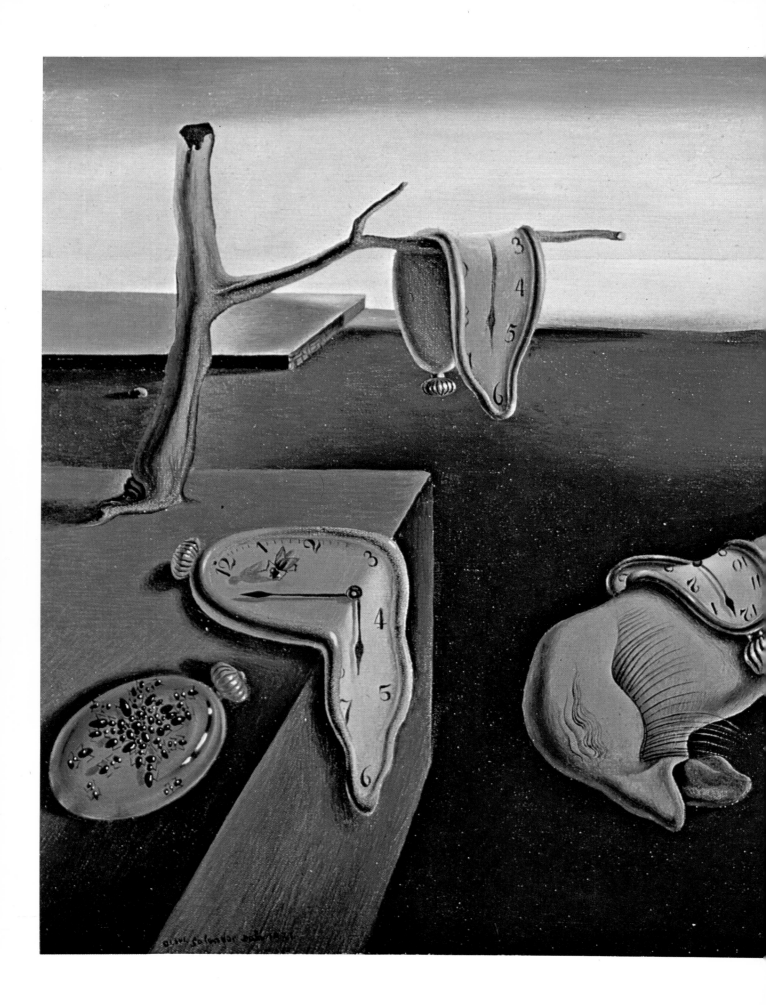

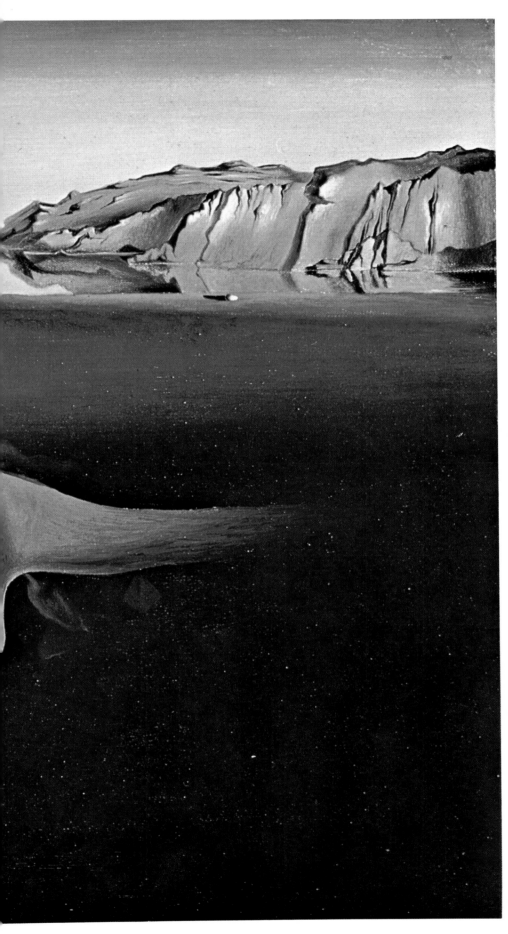

Plate 14
The Persistence of Memory
1931
Oil on canvas
$9\frac{1}{2} \times 13$ in (24.2 × 33 cm)
Museum of Modern Art, New
York

Dali has said that eating Camembert
cheese inspired the limp watches:
'Be persuaded that Salvador Dali's
famous limp watches are nothing
else than the tender, extravagant
and solitary paranoiac-critical Camembert of time and space.' This
image was to make its appearance
in many subsequent works.

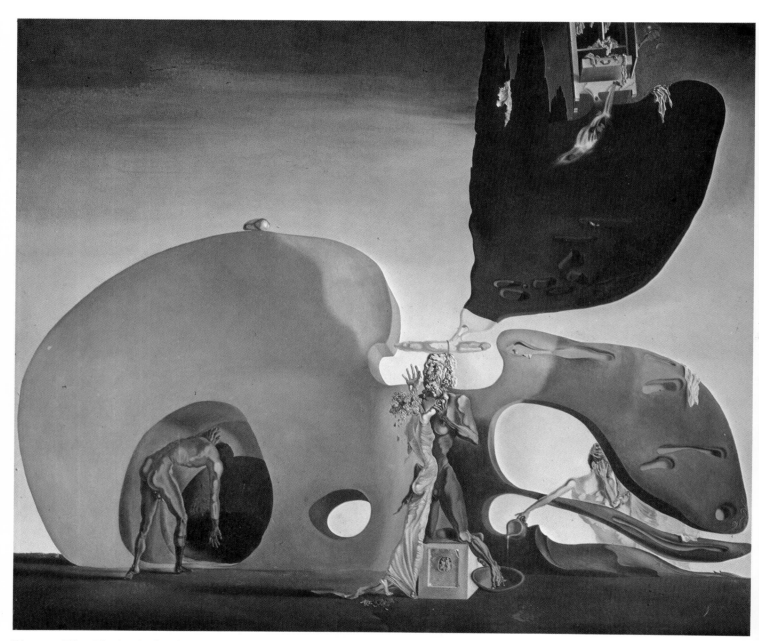

Plate 15 **The Birth of Liquid Desires**

formidable – a nude model who was to have live sea-urchins under each arm, several decomposed donkeys, a grand piano, a cut-off hand, three ants' nests and a cow's eye.

The winter of 1929 saw the first showing of *Un Chien Andalou*. Praised by the Surrealists for its dream sequences and arresting imagery, the audience had little stomach for a film that opened with a woman's eye being sliced by a razor in close-up. The following year saw their second film *L'Age d'Or* (*The Golden Age*) (plate 12), financed by the Vicomte de Noailles. Full of violence and revolt, it showed archbishops and bones among the rocks of Cape Creus, a blind man being ill-treated, a dog crushed to death, a son killed by his father, and a character from de Sade disguised as Christ. Riots broke out, with the right-wing pro-Hitler group, the 'Camelots du Roy', smashing up the cinema. The police intervened and further showings were banned.[1]

For all Dali's frenetic activity, the success which he so desperately sought did not come. It was an intolerable situation. Shunning his new-found friends to spend hours sitting in cafés or wandering the boulevards, he felt again the touch of madness. The following evening 'I thus hung my illness on the coathanger of the Gare d'Orsay ...' He caught a train for Spain.

Back in Cadaqués the recent events disappeared, replaced with the wonders and fantasies of childhood. Strange images, he tells us, took possession of his mind, rising enigmatically from out of the dark. The immediate thought was to make a painting to reproduce each image in all its clarity and as scrupulously as possible. It would be completely automatic, without conscious intervention, obeying only his authentic, biological desire. *The Lugubrious Game* (plate 6) – the title was suggested by Eluard – was Dali's first truly Surrealist painting. In his autobiography he wrote:

'This work, unusual and disconcerting in the highest degree, was by the very physiology of its elaboration far removed from the "Dadaist collage", which is always a poetic and *a posteriori* arrangement. It was also the contrary of Chirico's metaphysical painting, for here the spectator had perforce to believe in the earthy reality of the subject, which was one of an elementary and frenzied biological nature. And it was furthermore the contrary of the poetic softening of certain abstract paintings which continue stupidly, like blind moths, to bump into the extinguished lamps of the neo-Platonic light.

'I, then, and only I was the true Surrealist painter, at least according to the definition which its chief, André Breton, gave of Surrealism. Nevertheless, when Breton saw this painting, he hesitated for a long time before its scatological elements, for in the picture appeared a figure seen from behind, whose drawers were bespattered with excrement. The involuntary aspect of this element, so characteristic in psychopathological iconography, should have sufficed to enlighten him. But I was obliged to justify myself by saying that it was merely a simulacrum. No further questions were asked. But had I been

Plate 15
The Birth of Liquid Desires
1932
Oil on canvas
$44\frac{1}{4} \times 37\frac{1}{2}$ in (112 × 95 cm)
Peggy Guggenheim Collection, Venice

[1]For a detailed account of *Un Chien Andalou* and *L'Age d'Or* see J. H. Matthews, *Surrealism and Film*, The University of Michigan Press, Ann Arbor, 1971.

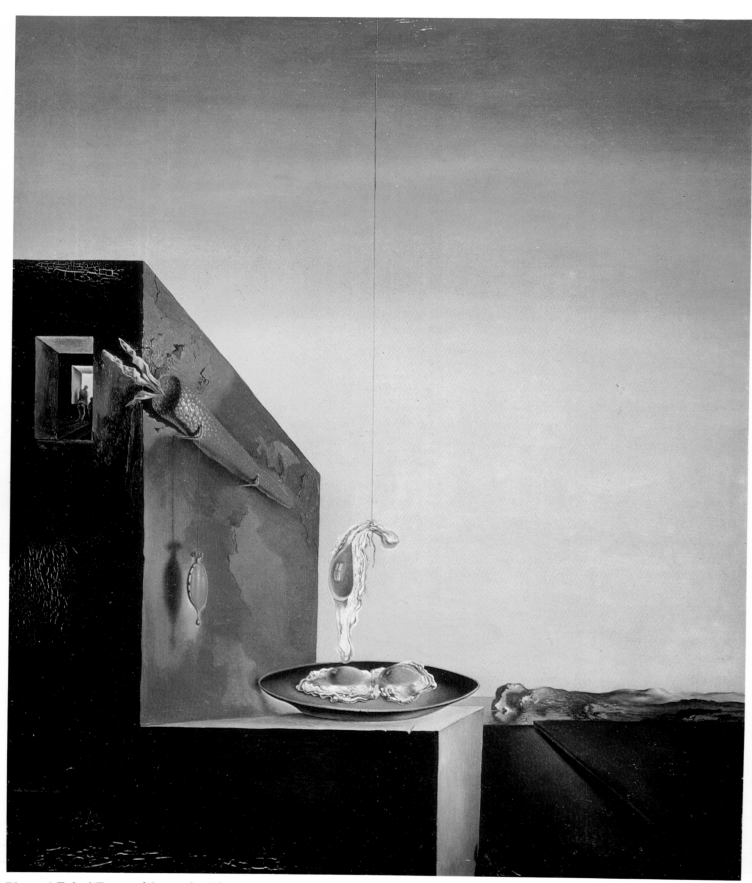

Plate 16 **Fried Eggs without the Plate**

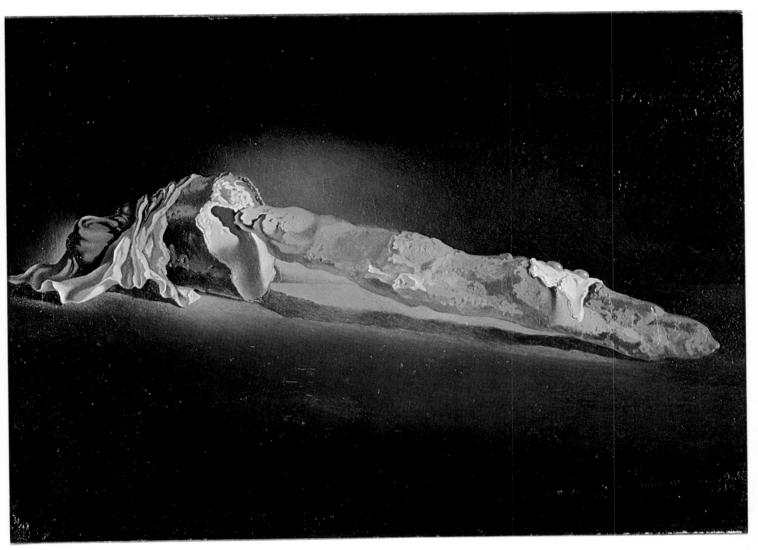

Plate 16
Fried Eggs without the Plate
Oeufs sur le Plat sans le Plat
1932
Oil on canvas
23¾ × 16½ in (60.4 × 42 cm)
Collection of Mr and Mrs
A. Reynolds Morse, Salvador Dali
Museum, Cleveland (Ohio)

The pun in the original French title
is untranslatable into English.

Plate 17
**Ordinary French Bread with
Two Fried Eggs, without a
Plate, on Horseback, Trying to
Sodomise a Crumb of
Portuguese Bread**
1932
Oil on wood
6¼ × 12⅝ in (16.8 × 32 cm)
Takahashi Shoji collection, Tokyo

The image of fried eggs was an
'ever-hallucinatory image' for Dali,
which he claimed to be able to
produce at will by putting pressure
on his closed eyes. Eggs appeared
in a number of works around this
period, including *Fried Eggs without
the Plate* (plate 16).

29

pressed, I should certainly have had to answer that it was the simulacrum of the excrement itself. This idealistic narrowness was, from my point of view, the fundamental "intellectual vice" of the early period of Surrealism. Hierarchies were established where there was no need for any. Between the excrement and a piece of rock crystal, by the very fact that they both sprang from the common basis of the unconscious, there could and should be no difference in category. And these were the men who denied the hierarchies of tradition!'[1]

During this period in Cadaqués, there was to be a deepening of his visionary imagination, an inextinguishable fecundity of experiments and an enrichment of his technique. His sympathies were now wholeheartedly with the Surrealists. The summer of 1929 saw not only *The Lugubrious Game* but also *Accommodations of Desire* (plate 8) in which he turned to collage, the pasting of photographic or engraved elements on to his canvas. He used this not as Picasso and the Cubists had done, as a formal means and an extension of the painter's palette,

Plate 18
Memory of the Child-Woman
1932
Oil on canvas
39 × 47¼ in (99 × 110 cm)
Private collection

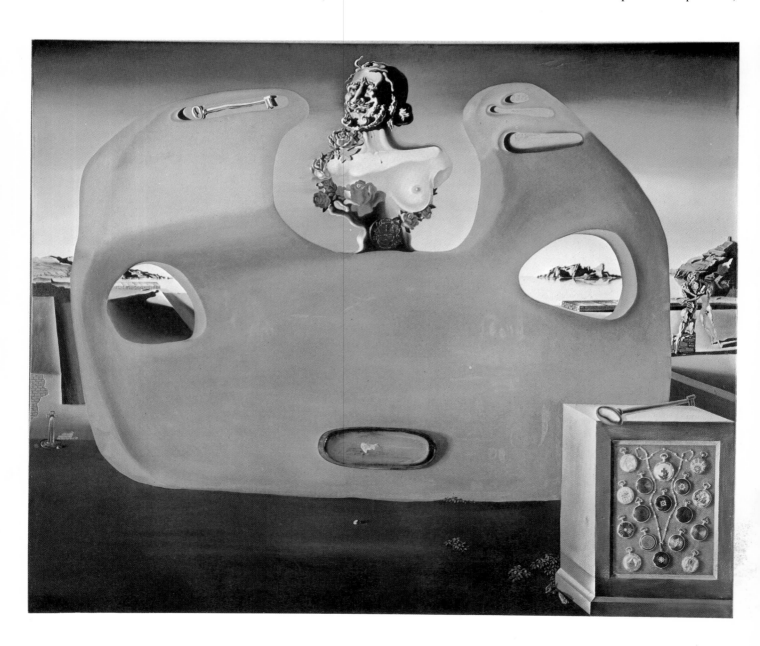

integrating the painted cuttings with the brushwork in a purely textural way. Instead he exploited the disruptive potential of collage. Rather than playing down the subject matter, he used it to dramatise the psychological and social objectives, with its pictorial aspect always used as a vehicle for the communication of ideas. Although the head of the lion is a photographic cut-out, the overall exactitude of the printed areas in the work is so perfect that we are confused by what is collage and what is paint.

Of the same year is *Illumined Pleasures* (plate 9) which clearly reveals his growing debt to de Chirico[2] in the framed painting within the painting and the unreal use of colour to suggest a dreamlike atmosphere. It is particularly noticeable for its photographic realism which gives such credibility to the most irrational subject matter. In his insistence on obeying the dictates of the unconscious, Dali set up his easel at the foot of the bed so that before going to sleep he could fix his mind on the unfinished painting to link his sleep with its further development. At other times he would 'wait whole hours

[1]This was written in the late 1940s, long after the break with Surrealism.

[2]In 1917 de Chirico produced a group of metaphysical interiors in which, against an architectural background, he painted framed pictures within an interior.

Plate 19
Giorgio de Chirico
The Philosophy of Conquest
1914
Art Institute of Chicago

Dali has often made use of de Chirico's deep perspective and the mystery of his shadows, as in *Nostalgic Echo, Illumined Pleasures* (plate 9) and *Outskirts of Paranoiac-Critical Town* (plate 34).

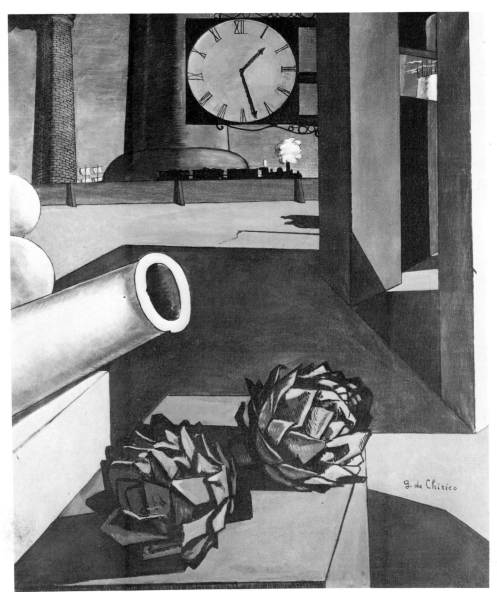

without any such images occurring. Then, not painting, I would remain in suspense ...' or would try by all means possible to simulate madness. Visions of 'three tiny curates running very fast in single file across a little Japanese gangplank ...'[1] would set him off into fits of laughter. Again, he imagined owls perched on peoples' heads, surmounted by pieces of excrement. Free from all reason, he recorded it all with maniacal care.

In the meantime, Camille Goemans arranged to put on his first Paris exhibition late in 1929. The terms were for Dali to receive 3,000 francs for all the works he produced during the summer. Goemans would take a percentage on the sales and have three canvases of his choice. It was an instant success with almost all the paintings sold at between six and twelve thousand francs. *The Lugubrious Game* was bought by the Vicomte de Noailles, who later was to acquire so many of his works.

It was not long before the Surrealists recognised the significant contribution that Dali could now make to the movement. His belief in the superiority of association, the omnipotence of dreams and the

[1] This image was later to be realised in the Dali-Buñuel film *L'Age d'Or*.

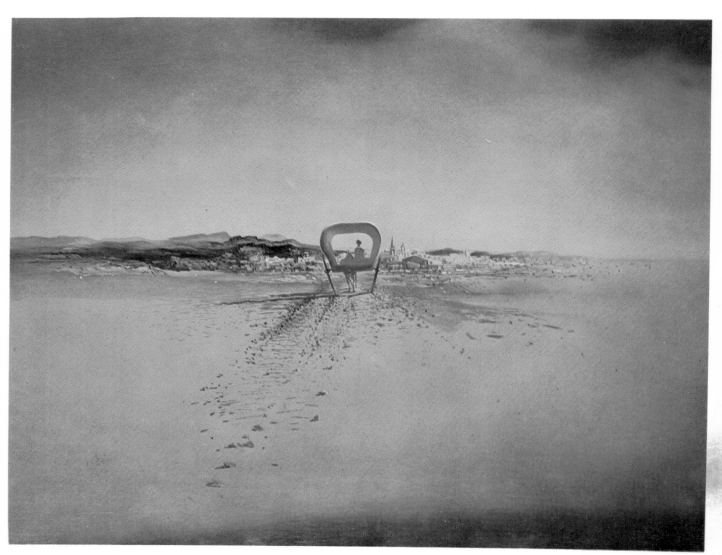

Plate 20 **The Phantom Cart**

element of chance were seen as means to an end and an instrument of exploration and discovery. His statement that he was completely uninterested in all aesthetic values and painterly qualities, concerned only with depicting the images of the irrational, was in line with Surrealism's avowed claim that the use of a technique was but a means to an end, that of reconciling man and the universe. During the following weeks Buñuel, Magritte and his wife, Paul Eluard and his wife Gala arrived in Cadaqués. They were distressed by his continuing fits of convulsive laughter and general mental state, and also concerned about his painting *The Lugubrious Game* (plate 6). Eluard suggested Gala approach him on the subject. Did the picture, with its realistic spattering of excrement on the man's back, and to which he showed a particular attachment, refer in any way to his life? Was he in fact a coprophagic? In any case it was felt that the work was weakened by its propaganda as a psychopathological document.

Dali assured her that he had no liking for that type of aberration, but did 'consider scatology as a terrorising element, just as I do blood, or my phobia for grasshoppers'.

This period saw the beginning of his great love for Gala. In his usual way he went to inordinate lengths to attract her. Taking his best shirt he cut it short enough to expose his navel, then tore it on the shoulder and the chest. The collar was entirely removed, his pants turned inside out. Shaving his armpits, they were then dyed with laundry blue. Not completely satisfied, he removed the blue and shaved until his armpits were bloody, then did the same to the knees. For perfume he could find only Eau de Cologne, which made him sick; so he boiled fish glue and water, adding some goat manure and a touch of aspic, making a paste which he rubbed all over his body. He was ready to meet her. Then he saw her through the window and realised that the whole get-up was a nuptial costume. Hurriedly changing, washing off the stench of the concoction as well as possible, he ran to meet her only to collapse at her feet in hysterical laughter.

Gala's initial reaction was not favourable. She thought him obnoxious and unbearable, yet a medium-like intuition told her that his hysteria was not gaiety nor scepticism, but fanaticism. They began to rely increasingly on each other. One day, when he threw himself at her feet, she cried out: 'My little boy! We shall never leave each other.'

Gala. She was born Elena Deluvina Diakanoff, in Russia. She was one of the most fascinating women around the Surrealists during those days. Most of them had been in love with her before her marriage to the poet, Paul Eluard, yet little is really known about her. Like an apparition she appears and disappears, leaving only a fleeting imprint that stirs our imagination. No one has written more about her than Dali. Many of his works are dedicated to her and are frequently signed with their entwined names. Yet she remains remote, always just out of our grasp. When the others returned to Paris, including Eluard, she remained with Dali in Cadaqués.

Plate 20
The Phantom Cart
1933
Oil on panel
6 × 8½ in (15.2 × 21.5 cm)
Edward James Foundation

One of Dali's more lyrical works which preceded the 'Beach at Rosas' series of 1934–1936. The two figures seated in the cart are also the buildings of the distant town, suggesting that the cart has already reached its destination.

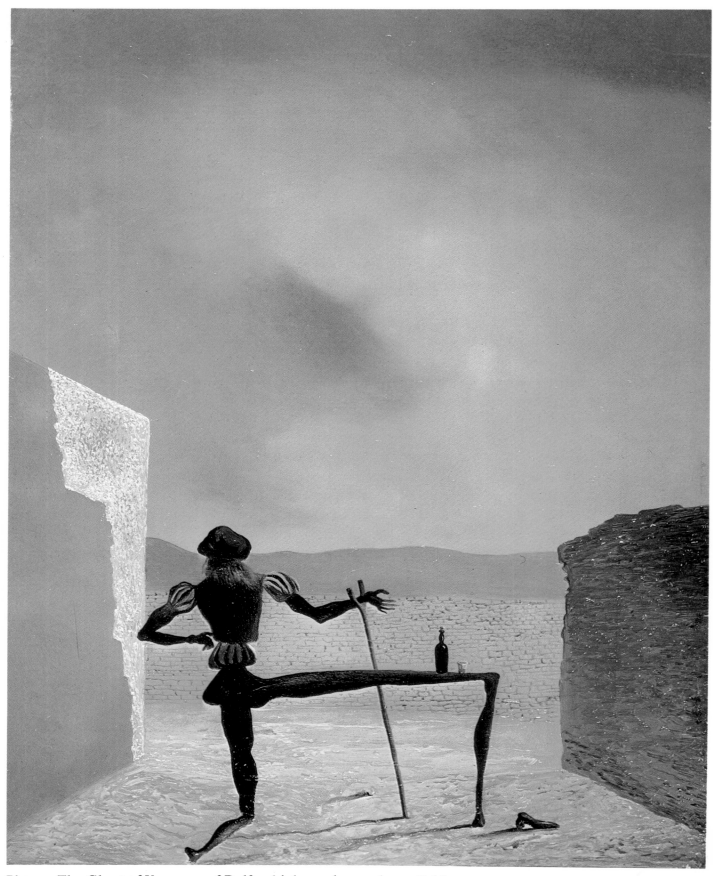

Plate 21 **The Ghost of Vermeer of Delft which can be used as a Table**

Dali was now working on a portrait of Paul Eluard and two other large canvases. One was to create a scandal. It represented, he tells us, 'a large head, livid as wax, the cheeks very pink, the eyelashes long, and the impressive nose pressed against the earth. This face has no mouth, and in its place was stuck an enormous grasshopper. The grasshopper's belly was decomposed, and full of ants. Several of these ants scurried across the space that should have been filled by the mouth of the great anguished face, whose head terminated in architecture and ornamentations of the style of 1900.' He called the painting *The Great Masturbator*.

His works all packed for his forthcoming exhibition, he again set off for Paris. This time he was to join the Surrealist group.

It is perhaps necessary to pause for a moment while we consider the development of Surrealist painting and the position it had arrived at around the time of Dali's intervention. While it would be impossible to summarise here all the various manifestations that determined the principles on which it rests and continues to build, we can consider some of its fundamental aims.

The first theoretical foundations of Surrealism were laid in 1924, the year of the first Surrealist manifesto, under the direction of André Breton. Surrealism dedicated itself to a far more systematic revision of values and an attitude towards the subconscious as the essential source of all art, following the disruptive and anarchistic action of Dada, which had died in 1922. As a result, a definition was made, dictionary style: 'SURREALISM, n, Pure psychic automatism, by which it is intended to express, verbally, in writing, or by other means, the real process of thought. Thought's dictation, in the absence of all control exercised by reason and outside all aesthetic or moral preoccupations. ENCYCL. philos. Surrealism rests in the belief in the superior reality of certain forms of association neglected heretofore, in the omnipotence of the dream and in the disinterested play of thought. It tends definitely to do away with all other psychic mechanisms and to substitute itself for them in the solution of the principal problems of life.'

The essential spirit of Surrealism, at that time, was clearly formulated. It was a purely intuitive period. 'I believe,' said Breton, 'in the future resolution of the states of dream and reality, in appearance so contradictory, in a sort of absolute reality, or *surréalité*, if I may so call it.'

No conception of Surrealist painting existed then. In fact it was difficult to see how it could transcend 'all aesthetic . . . preoccupations'. Only in automatic writing, in fantasies and states of hallucination could the stream of consciousness emerge. Indeed, Pierre Naville, in 1925, expressed the view that there could be no such thing as Surrealist painting. The whole idea was a contradiction in terms. Breton did not see the definition as quite so rigid. In the same year he published a book, under the still hesitant title *Surrealism and Painting*, in which he declared that 'Painting could supply the rhythmic unity', and there could be an art as 'an instrument of discovery'.

Plate 21
The Ghost of Vermeer of Delft which can be used as a Table
1934
Oil on panel
$7\frac{1}{8} \times 5\frac{1}{2}$ in (18 × 14 cm)
Collection of Mr and Mrs A. Reynolds Morse, Salvador Dali Museum, Cleveland (Ohio)

Dali's obsession with food and furniture probably prompted this painting, as well as his respect for the art of Vermeer. He has said of this work, 'A spectre that could be used as a table: an eminently eucharistic idea for a painting'.

Plate 22
Atmospheric Skull Sodomising a Grand Piano
1934
Oil on panel
5½ × 7 in (14 × 17.8 cm)
Collection of Mr and Mrs
A. Reynolds Morse, Salvador Dali
Museum, Cleveland (Ohio)

The French for 'a grand piano' ('*un piano à queue*') means literally 'a piano with a tail'. The idea for this painting came to Dali during those moments between sleep and waking. The beach scene is an accurate reproduction of the view from his house.

Surrealist identity would hinge on the methodological and iconographic relevance of the picture to the main ideas of the movement – that is, to automatism and the 'dream image'. The automatism of painters like Miró and Masson was the equivalent of the verbal free association which the writer practised. The artist had merely to let his brush wander freely over the surface. 'Rather than setting out to paint something,' Miró explained, 'I begin painting, and as I paint the picture begins to assert itself, or suggest itself under my brush. The form becomes the sign for a woman or a bird as I work . . . The first stage is free, unconcious . . .'

As we see, Surrealism from the beginning excluded the rational and the logical in favour of the irrational. Painters were urged not to draw their inspiration from reality, but from a 'purely interior model' which was defined in those painters who genuinely rediscovered the reason for painting. 'These,' said Breton, 'were Picasso, Max Ernst, Masson, Miró, Tanguy, Arp, Picabia and Man Ray. It was not the artistic quality that was important, but its Surrealist quality. Only its hidden content was of value. This motivation reveals the difference between Surrealist painting and other forms of artistic creation under the sway of aesthetic considerations.'

While automatism still remains today the best-known method of tapping the imaginative resources, the Surrealists were not unaware of the inherent weaknesses in the process. Breton, speaking of the definition of Surrealism made in 1924, admitted '. . . that I deceived myself at the time in advocating the use of an automatic thought not only removed from all control exercised by the reason, but also disengaged from "all aesthetic or moral preoccupations". It should at least have said: "conscious aesthetic or moral preoccupations".' Fascinating though the automatic approach might be, the image has a habit of repeating itself indefinitely. An element of monotony and repetition creeps into unconscious experience. By 1928 many of the Surrealist painters were in the process of working out a method by which the discoveries made by chance could be completed by the intervention of the artist himself, in order to achieve the full realisation of what was inspired by the automatic process. In other words, some degree of control would be necessary.

Dali shared the Surrealists' faith in adapting the automatic processes to painting, in recording the involuntary images inspired by dreams. He also saw that, for the imagery to achieve its full potentiality, it had to be developed in a fully conscious way. It did not mean that he arrested the process of free association by which one image suggested another, but that he sought to elaborate his psychic revelations with all the precision and artistic skill at his command, in a conscious and deliberate manner. 'Handmade photography' was the term he used to describe his technique, by which he meant that his painting would be indistinguishable from photography and therefore more believable. Even the size of many of these paintings was no larger than the average photograph.

The Freudian basis of Surrealism was clearly defined between the

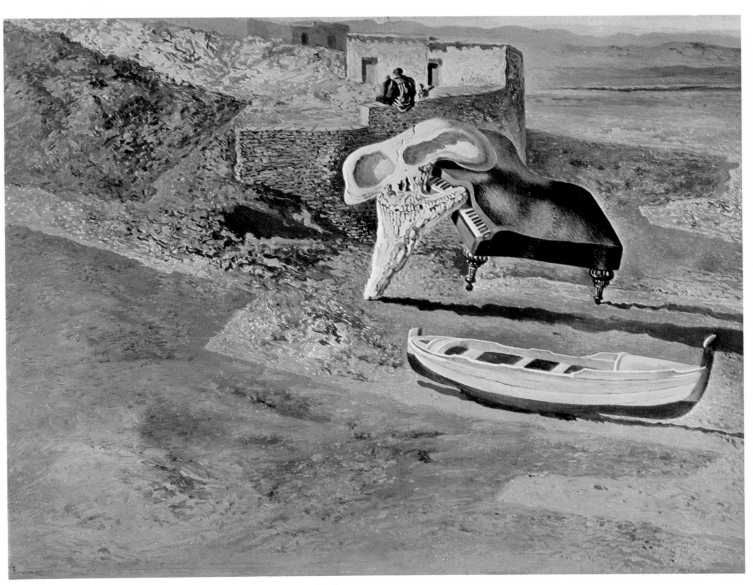

Plate 22 **Atmospheric Skull Sodomising a Grand Piano**

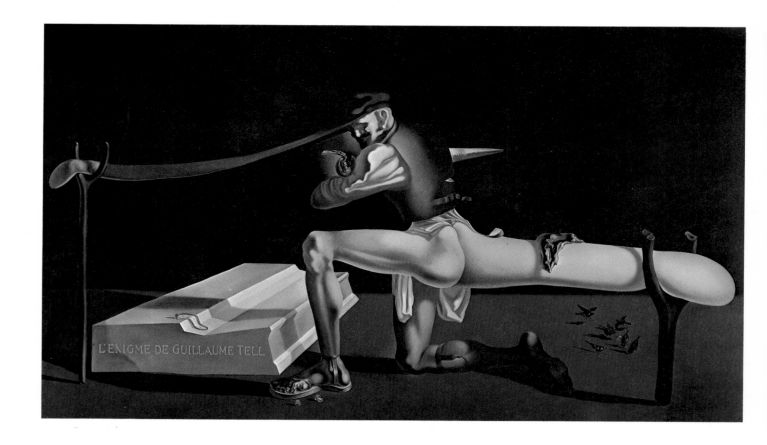

Plate 23
The Enigma of William Tell
1934
Oil on canvas
78¾ × 128 in (200 × 325 cm)
National Museum, Stockholm

The legend of William Tell was re-interpreted by Dali as one of incestuous mutilation. Although devoted to his father, Dali revolted against his authority, a situation which eventually led to his being thrown out of his father's home. The fond relationship between father and son in the legend was to become a thematic obsession for a number of important works: *William Tell*, painted in 1930, and *The Old Age of William Tell* of 1931. This particular painting, in which Lenin appears trouserless and with an extended buttock, combined with Dali's reactionary political tendencies, was to bring about his first break with the Surrealists.

Some years later Dali made the following comment about the painting: 'William Tell, a fatherly phantasm, has placed a mutton chop on my head, indicating the desire to eat the infant Dali, whom he carries in his arms.'

first manifesto of 1924 and the second manifesto of 1929. Technically, the paintings of that period fall roughly into two groups. The first is the intuitive, spontaneous approach of Masson and Miró, with its allegiance to dreams, folly and the incoherent. Breton proposed the unbridled imagination, and if it contradicted that which was known, all the better. The second type of Surrealist painting draws on a meticulously realistic technique by which the identity of the object is firmly designated. In this category is found the art of such painters as Magritte, Brauner and Dali. Yet there is one important difference in Dali's use of his technical ability, namely that he put it at the service of automatism and passivity. At the same time he was to revive, with his convincingly illusionist realism, the theory of painting as an illustrative medium and to champion a return of the anecdote to art. It was a contribution of major importance to Surrealism at that time and gave a new impetus to experiments that were still at a tentative stage.

Breton may have been aware, even that early, of the risks that Dali might face. In his introduction to the 1929 exhibition he wrote: 'Dali is like a man who hesitates between talent and genius, or as one might once have said, between vice and virtue. He is one of those who arrive from so far away that one barely has time to see them enter — only enter. He takes his place, without saying a word, in a system of interference.' He continues in a later paragraph: 'On the other hand there is hope: hope that not everything will become dark even so, that the admirable voice which is Dali's will not break when it reaches one's ears, even though certain "materialists" are anxious that the sound of it should be confused with the creaking of his patent leather shoes ...'[1] Whatever doubts were felt, the importance accorded to him was clearly stated: 'With the coming of Dali, it is perhaps the first time that the mental windows have been opened really wide, so that one can feel oneself gliding up towards the wild sky's trap.'[2]

The originality of Dali, the revolutionary critical interpretation he brought to bear upon familiar works of art, his translating hallucinations and dreams into a concrete reality, and his fascination with all forms of aberration were all essential to Surrealist aims at that time. His understanding of Freud, on which so much of his work was to be based, led to the development of his theories of the 'paranoiac method'. In his book *The Visible Woman* he described it as 'a spontaneous method of irrational knowledge based upon the critical and systematic objectification of delirious associations and interpretations'. In simple terms it was a form of image interpretation, in which the spectator sees in a picture a different image depending on the imaginative ability of the onlooker. For instance, one might see, in a stain on the wall, a face, a castle or a galloping horse. A postcard of a group of negroes sitting around their hut had only to be seen from another angle to become a portrait of André Breton. (Breton insisted it was of the Marquis de Sade.) It was to become the subject for a future painting.

Not unrelated to the paranoiac method is Lautréamont's image, 'beautiful as the chance meeting upon a dissecting table of a sewing machine and an umbrella'. In Freudian terms we recognise the sewing machine as a woman, the umbrella as a man and the dissecting table as a bed. The sewing machine and the umbrella will make love.

Dali envisaged the possibilities of giving objective value on the plane of reality to his world of irrational experiences. The paranoiac-critical activity became a system of revealing images and associations. Like other methods used by the Surrealists, it was a means of forcing inspiration.[3] The interpretative system of paranoiac-critical activity led Dali to transform Millet's *Angelus* into a painting of extreme eroticism. He found that the man on the left was using his hat to hide his turgescent sex, that the woman was pregnant, and that the pitchfork, thrust into the ground alongside the open sack of potatoes, symbolised the male sex and the sack of potatoes the female. Dali maintained that the immense success of the picture, its devout subject matter apart, was entirely due to its latent content.

He was to produce a number of pictures on this theme; for instance, *Gala and the 'Angelus' of Millet Immediately Preceding the Arrival of the Conic Anamorphoses*, illustrated in *Le Surréalisme au Service de la Revolution*, No. 6, 1933, and *Meditation upon the Harp*. Both executed between 1932 and 1935, they are two examples in which he applies the method to the obsessional character of the *Angelus*.

Another artistic theme was launched when he discovered in the legend of William Tell, not the filial devotion that people saw, but incestuous mutilation. It is explored in *William Tell, The Enigma of William Tell* (plate 23) and *The Old Age of William Tell*.

[1] Introduction to the catalogue of the first Dali exhibition, Galerie Goemans, 1929.

[2] Ibid.

[3] The Surrealists made use of a number of automatic processes for this purpose. Decalcomania, or transfer, developed by Dominguez, is a technique in which paint is spread on a sheet of glazed paper, then covered with a similar sheet. After exerting pressure it is slowly lifted, revealing the effect of strange rock formations, mysterious grottoes and coral effects. It was later used by Max Ernst in such paintings as *Napoleon in the Desert, The Eye of Silence* and *Europe after the Rain*, around 1937. Fumage was invented by Paalen: a canvas, or any surface, is moved at random above a lighted candle, the smoke being allowed to make marks on the surface. Frottage, used by Max Ernst in 1925, is a matter of applying a sheet of paper or canvas over an uneven surface or object and rubbing with a pencil or crayon, as children do with coins. Ernst's first results were published under the title of *Natural History*. It is important to remember that all these processes were subjected to conscious control by the artist, once the discoveries made by chance were revealed.

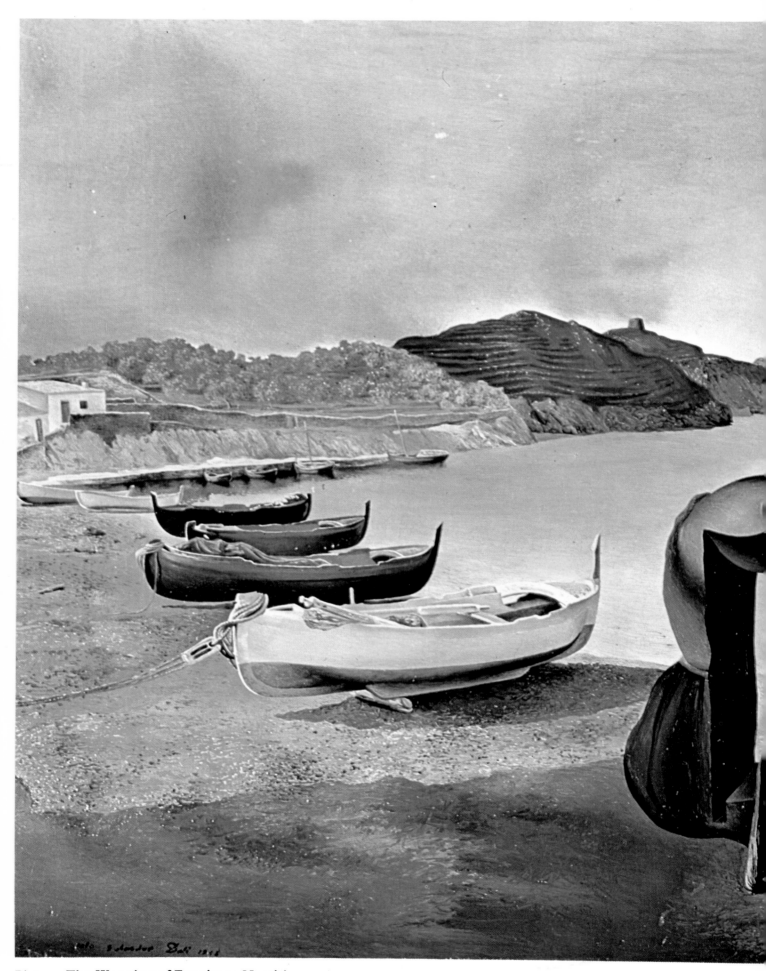

Plate 24 **The Weaning of Furniture-Nutrition**

40

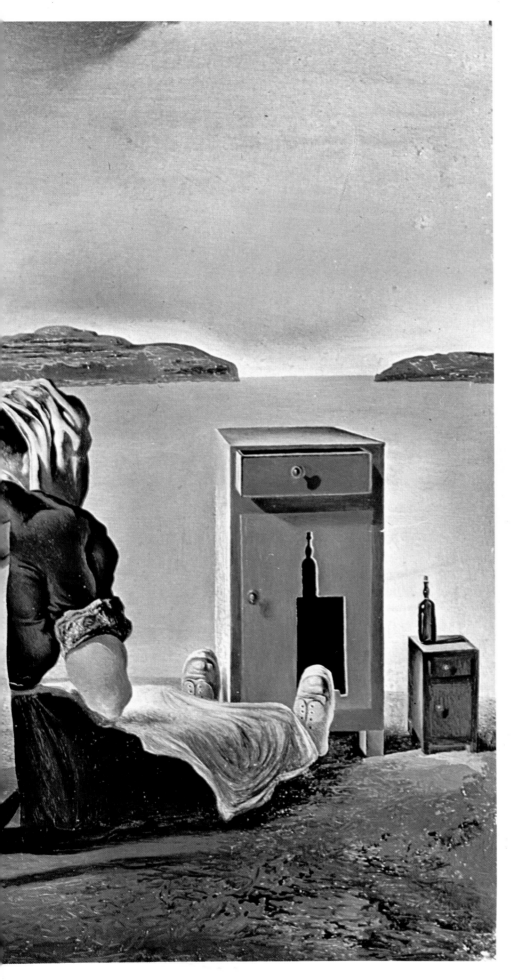

Plate 24
**The Weaning of Furniture-
Nutrition**
1934
Oil on panel
7 × 9½ in (17.8 × 24.2 cm)
Collection of Mr and Mrs
A. Reynolds Morse, Salvador Dali
Museum, Cleveland (Ohio)

The back view of the woman is a
composite of Dali's childhood nurse
and a half-mad fisherwoman named
Lidia who lived at Port Lligat and
from whom Dali bought a dilapi-
dated fishing hut from which was
created his present home. The space
cut from the body of the nurse con-
forms to that of the larger chest
which, taken from the woman,
might therefore be considered
edible. Note the baby's feeding
bottle on the small chest.

Plate 25 *overleaf*
L'Omelette Baveuse
1934
Oil on canvas
Private collection

The architecture and ornamentation of Art Nouveau had a profound
effect on Dali between the years
1930 and 1934, as can be seen in the
ectoplasmic forms in this painting.
The irridescent tonality of certain
works of the Surrealist painter Yves
Tanguy also impressed him at this
time.

Plate 26 *overleaf*
**Skull with its Lyrical Append-
age Leaning on a Night Table
which should have the
Temperature of a Cardinal's
Nest**
1934
Oil on panel
9½ × 7½ in (24 × 19 cm)
Private collection

Here a given reality is made to
suggest another. The piano keys
metamorphose into the teeth of a
skull. Such image interpretation
was, claimed Dali, entirely due to
his 'paranoiac-critical method'.

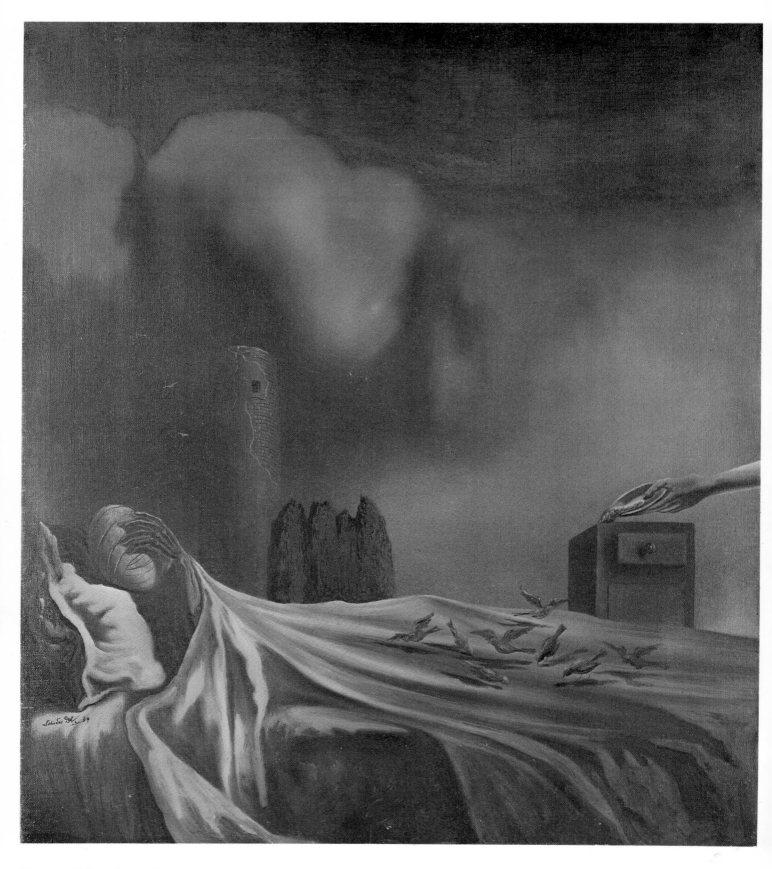

Plate 25 **L'Omelette Baveuse**

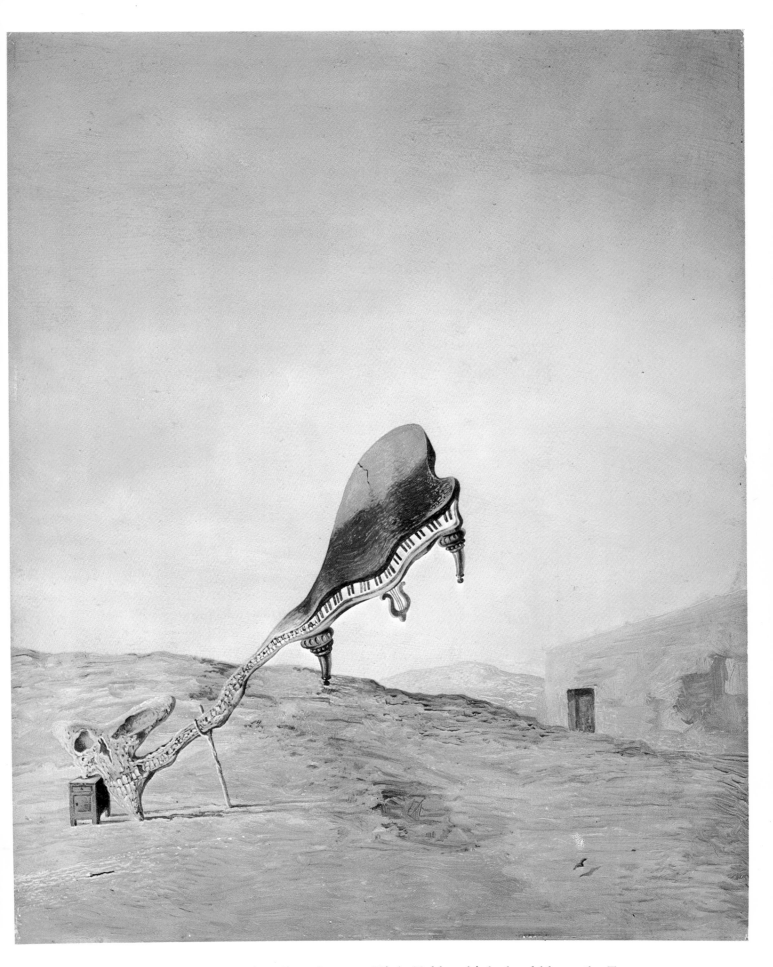

Plate 26 **Skull with its Lyrical Appendage Leaning on a Night Table which should have the Temperature of a Cardinal's Nest**

Dali's ineffable talent for parading his irrational delirium, his lurid taste for the sensational, was working overtime. He asserted his taste for chromolithographs (a picture printed in colours from stone) as 'the least accidental imitations of nature', and threw light on his own work which was of an 'instantaneous photography in colours and with images that are super-fine, extravagant, extra-plastic, extra-pictorial, unexplored, super-pictorial, super-plastic, deceptive, hyper-normal, feeble and of concrete irrationality'.

It is of course possible to accept the iconography of his work, as Dali himself would insist, without asking what each detail might mean. Yet we know from his own account, not only of his childhood, but of the interpretative studies he has made of Millet, William Tell, the Pre-Raphaelites and others, that there is evidence of a specific meaning behind most of the imagery that finds it way into the paintings. Some, to which he attaches particular importance, are also unforgettable, like the crutches and limp watches. Others, more alarming, he tried to canalise by putting them down on canvas. Grasshoppers, for which he had a morbid fear, identified with dislike for his father. Excrement was seen as 'the terrorising element'. Teeth are a Freudian sex symbol. Blood, forced into his eyes by hanging or swinging his head, provoked retinal illusions. Putrefaction had the hard light of gems. Death he saw as always being beautiful, just as eroticism must always be ugly. Implements, such as sharp instruments, are symbolic of mutilation. He considered that the three cardinal images of life were excrement, blood and putrefaction. 'We have long since learned to recognise the image of desire in images of terror,' said David Gascoyne.[1]

Since his early childhood, Dali was drawn to Vermeer of Delft. No painter has had such a devoted disciple, and Vermeer is probably the only painter he has ever made a copy of. According to Fleur Cowles,[2] the banker-collector Robert Lehman asked him to copy a Vermeer. Dali assured him it was impossible, but in the early 1960s, some twenty years later, in a special room set aside in the Louvre, after exhaustive tests and analysis of colours and pigments, minute study of the way paint was applied down to the width of the brush required, Dali went through a number of violent intellectual efforts to put himself in a state of receptivity. Suddenly he claimed to discover something extraordinary in the painting, which should not have been there. Immediately the experts gathered around with their magnifying glasses, until one discovered the hair from a paint brush hidden between the brush strokes, and the source of Dali's discomfort was revealed. Relieved, he then sat before his canvas and proceeded to draw a rhinoceros horn, in the structure of which he saw the origin of all life. The image recurred in a number of works, including *The Maximum Speed of Raphael's Madonna*; its perfect logarithmic spiral has Platonic implications for Dali.

The influence of Vermeer on his own work is to be seen in a number of paintings: *The Image Disappears*, and more directly in *The Ghost of Vermeer of Delft which can be used as a Table* (plate 21).

[1] *A Short Survey of Surrealism*, Cobden-Sanderson, 1936.

[2] *The Case of Salvador Dali*, 1959.

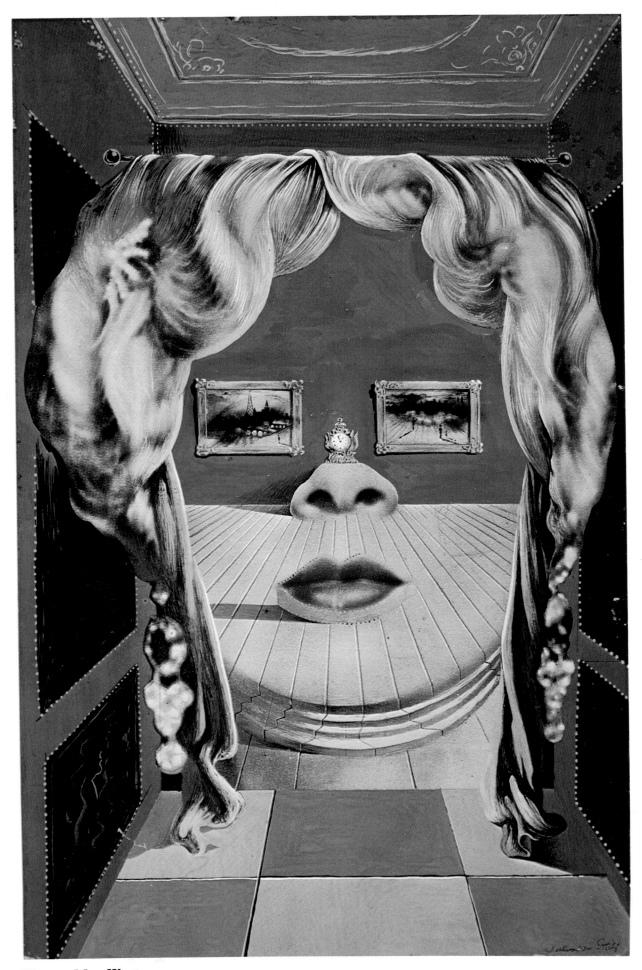

Plate 27 **Mae West**

Food has always been one of Dali's obsessions.[1] It occurs repeatedly in his autobiography: the prologue opens with, 'At the age of six I wanted to be a cook.' Such words as 'spinach', 'shellfish', 'sturgeon', 'cannibalism', 'bones' and 'caviar' are frequently used to describe painting. It led him to paint a portrait of Gala with two lamb chops on her shoulder, as well as *The Weaning of Furniture-Nutrition* (plate 24). Cooking turkey without killing it was one of his culinary refinements, and once he conceived the idea of making a table of egg-white so that it could be eaten. 'Cooking is very close to painting,' he insists. His devotion to food and Vermeer might explain why *The Ghost of Vermeer* (plate 21) suggests that it could be used as a dining table. If Vermeer has top marks in his gallery of painters, Velásquez runs him a close second, failing only in inspiration and mystery.[2] Applying his paranoiac-critical facility, he saw the apparition of Velásquez's Infanta in the top of a Hindu temple. More significantly, it is Velásquez's technical brilliance and richness of colour that are the lyrical inspiration for *Apparition of Face and Fruit-dish on a*

[1] *Les Diners de Gala,* with 136 recipes by Dali, has been published by Felicie Inc.

[2] *Fifty Secrets of Magic Craftsmanship,* Salvador Dali, 1948.

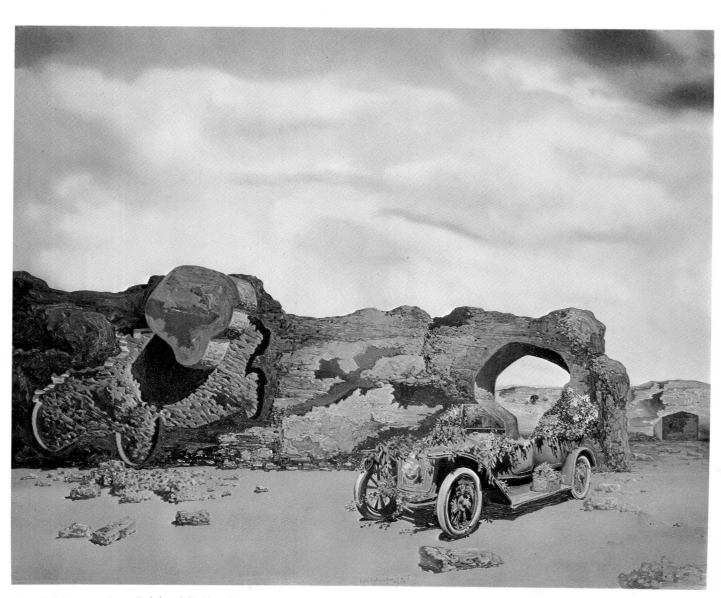

Plate 28 **Paranoiac-Critical Solitude**

Beach (plate 43). The painting is also an exploration into the use of the multiple image. The base of the fruit-dish is a back view of his childhood nurse to form the nose and mouth of the face, while the fruit and the coastline are metamorphosed into a dog.

History provides many such examples of the fantastic in art: distorted perspective, composite images, Bosch's highly personal visions, and the use of the double image by the late 16th-century painter Arcimboldo (plate 41). They were all put to a use by the Surrealists who had first rejected the rational basis on which these techniques were founded. Tearing away the curtain, they demonstrated that every form of the strange and mad could work in the cause of art and transport it outside its own limits. Dali's acceptance of every form of madness took him further than the other Surrealists. By simulating the disordered mind of the paranoiac, he became hypersensitive to hidden appearances and counter-appearances, seeing not two or three images but a sequence of images limited only by the mind's capacity. In *The Endless Enigma* six concealed images are represented in the painting. Less complex is *Old Age, Adolescence, Infancy*. Dali maintained that the delirious image suggested by an initial object might be the true reality. In *La Femme Visible* he wrote: 'I challenge materialists to enquire into the more complex problem as to which of these images has the highest probability of existence if the intervention of desire is taken into account.' The 'omnipotence of desire,' said Breton, 'has remained, since the beginning, Surrealism's sole act of faith.' The intensity of Dali's hallucinatory powers makes others believe in the reality of what he sees. In truth he could say that the putrefaction of a donkey can be considered as 'the hard and blinding flash of new gems'.

One of his more subtle uses of the double image is to be seen in the painting entitled *Spain* (plate 42). The group of horsemen and figures

Plate 28
Paranoiac-Critical Solitude
1935
Oil on panel
$7\frac{1}{2} \times 9\frac{1}{8}$ in (19 × 23 cm)
Edward James Foundation

Dali's dislike of all mechanical things led him to declare in his manifesto, *Declaration of the Independence of the Imagination and of the Rights of Man to his own Madness*: 'Only the violence and duration of your hardened dream can resist the hideous mechanical civilisation that is your enemy . . .'; and again: 'The history of the true creative artist is filled with the abuses and encroachments by means of which an absolute tyranny is imposed by the industrial mind over the new creative ideas of the poetic mind.'

The treatment of the car in this painting is characteristic of his contempt for the mechanical and for industrialism. Here the vehicle has been excavated fossil-like from the rock.

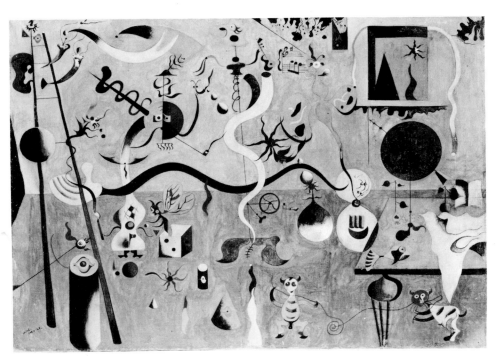

Plate 29
Joan Miró
The Carnival of Harlequin
1924–25
Albright-Knox Art Gallery,
Buffalo (N.Y.)

Miró was one of the first Surrealist painters. His work represents the intuitive, spontaneous approach as opposed to the realistic, which Dali was to introduce into Surrealism in 1929.

in combat, forming the face of the woman, owes an unmistakeable debt to Leonardo, another painter of the past whom he now admired. They both shared a common foundation of inventiveness. And Dali was undoubtedly familiar with Freud's study of Leonardo, as well as that artist's advice to look at the damp stains on walls in which one might see all kinds of strange and imaginary images.

'The abject misery of abstract creation'[1] is the chapter heading to Dali's attack on abstract art. He saw in it a lack of philosophic and general culture and evidence of mental debility, offering us 'upon the fresh optimism of their shiny paper the soup of the abstract aesthetic, which really and truly is even worse than the cold and colossally sordid vermicelli soups of neo-theism, which even the most convulsively hungry cats would not go near'.

As an antidote to its influence and to that of Negro art, which Picasso and other painters were extolling in Paris, Dali upheld the decoration and architecture of 'Art Nouveau', which he considered as 'the psychopathological end-product of the Greco-Roman decadence', finding in the ornamentation of the entrances to the Paris

[1] *The Conquest of the Irrational.*

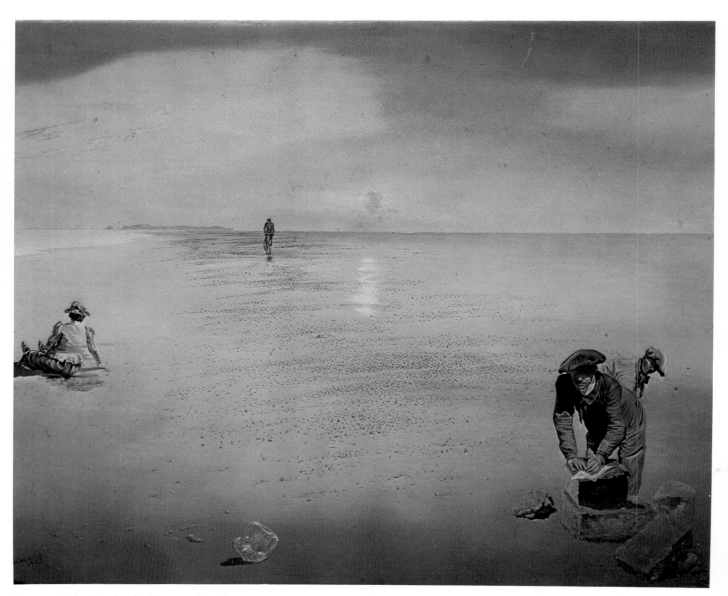

Plate 30 **Medianimic-Paranoiac Image**

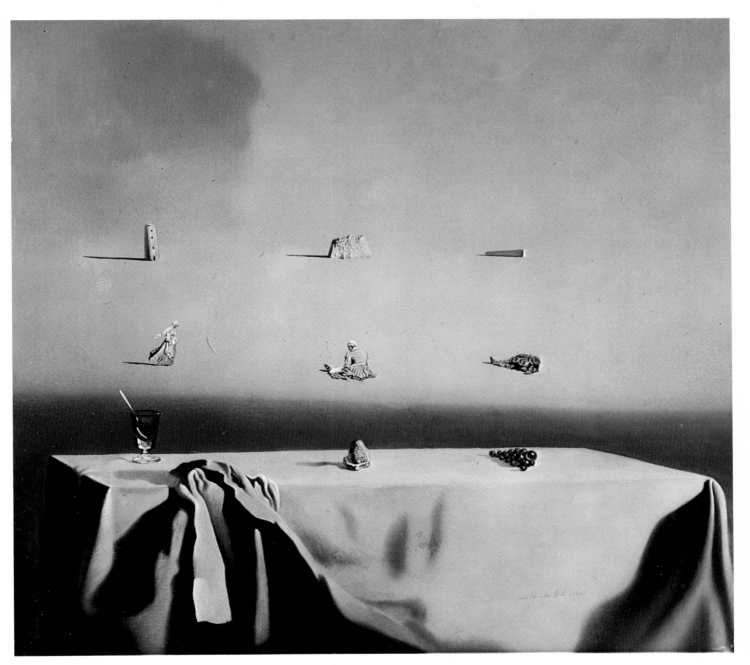

Plate 30
Medianimic-Paranoiac Image
1935
Oil on panel
$7\frac{1}{2} \times 9\frac{1}{8}$ in (19 × 23 cm)
Edward James Foundation

Another painting of the Rosas series in which the fixtures take on a phantom-like effect.

Plate 31
Morphological Echo
1936
Oil on panel
12 × 13 in (30.5 × 33 cm)
Collection of Mr and Mrs
A. Reynolds Morse, Salvador Dali Museum, Cleveland (Ohio)

Plate 32
Lobster-Telephone
1936
12 × 6 × 3 in (30 × 15 × 7 cm)
Edward James Foundation

Dali made a number of Surrealist objects for his English patron, Edward James, including the famous 'Lobster-Telephone'. It illustrates his fascination with giving life to the inanimate.

Plate 33
Three Young Surrealist Women Holding in their Arms the Skins of an Orchestra
1936
Oil on canvas
21¼ × 25⅝ in (54 × 65 cm)
Collection of Mr and Mrs
A. Reynolds Morse, Salvador Dali Museum, Cleveland (Ohio)

Plate 34
Outskirts of Paranoiac-Critical Town
1936
Oil on panel
18⅛ × 26 in (46 × 66 cm)
Edward James Foundation

The outline of the distant bell tower is duplicated in the foreground structure, through which is seen the skipping girl who also becomes the bell in the tower. Dali made a painting of this detail in 1935, called *Nostalgic Echo*. There is also a portrait of Gala holding up a bunch of grapes.

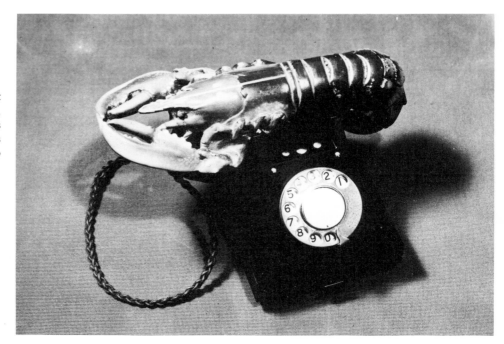

[1] Equally compulsive are the architectural structures of the Postman Cheval, who built his dream palace at Hauterives in France. Between 1879 and 1912 he collected stones in his postman's bag and laboriously over the years constructed his dream.

Metro a wrought iron vegetation full of mystery, eroticism and perversity. The imaginative dream structures of Antonio Gaudí in Barcelona, houses 'created for madmen, for erotomaniacs', were very familiar to Dali. The Parc Güell, and the Basilica of the Church of the Holy Family suggested 'in the most material way the persistence of dreams in the face of reality'.[1]

Many of the 'undulant-convulsive' forms in his paintings between 1930 and 1934 are traceable to the ornamental elements of the 1900 'Modern Style'. In the faces of these hysterical sculptures he saw those madwomen, treated by Dr Charcot, at the mental hospital of Saltpetrière.

The treatment of what gives all the appearance of petrified hair on two images in *The Font* has the delirium associated with the more extreme excesses of that style, and he also made significant use of its compositional motifs. The painting shows, too, his growing interest in the emotive value of deep perspective that he saw in certain canvases of de Chirico. But whereas de Chirico was motivated by the mystery hiding behind normal relationships, Dali evokes a delirious world of clinical irrationality bathed in an irridescent light. What he does share with de Chirico is the ability to project his apparent dislocations with the same acceptability, in spite of the inordinate nature of the imagery. *The Invisible Man*, which he started in 1929, did not escape the influence of Art Nouveau, recognisable in the treatment of the 'vaginal head' of the figure, as well as the sensuous ornamentation of the foreground.

There is little doubt that Dali's theories and plastic involvement with this style led to a revival of interest and a reappraisal of the movement. Nothing would have pleased him more than the public reaction in 1895 to the first Art Nouveau posters of Alphonse Mucha: 'le délire ... le délire de la laideur' ('delirium ... delirium of the

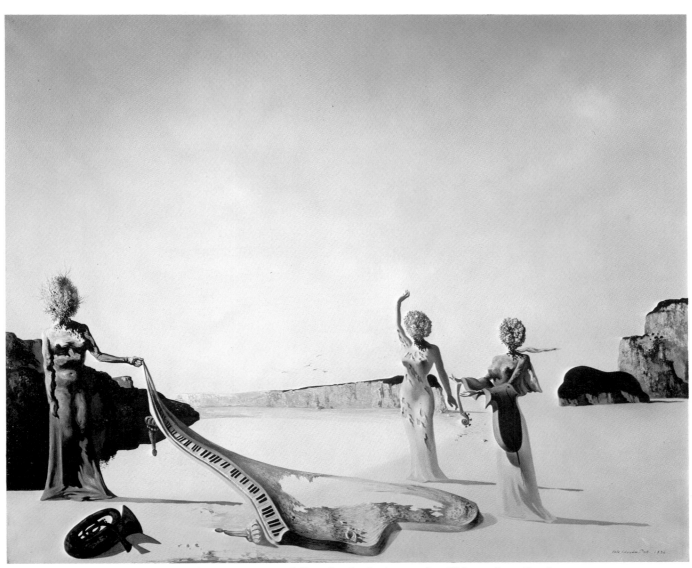

Plate 33 **Three Young Surrealist Women Holding in their Arms the Skins of an Orchestra**

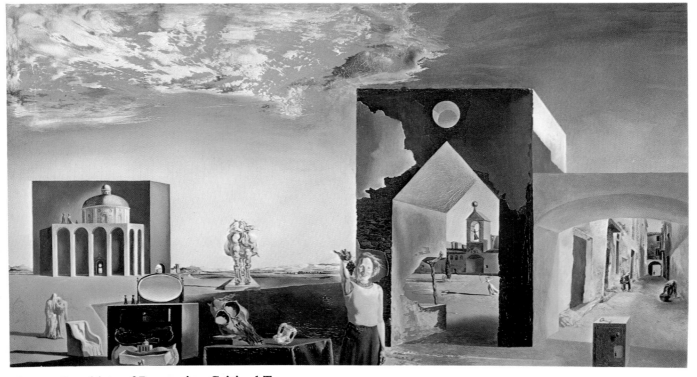

Plate 34 **Outskirts of Paranoiac-Critical Town**

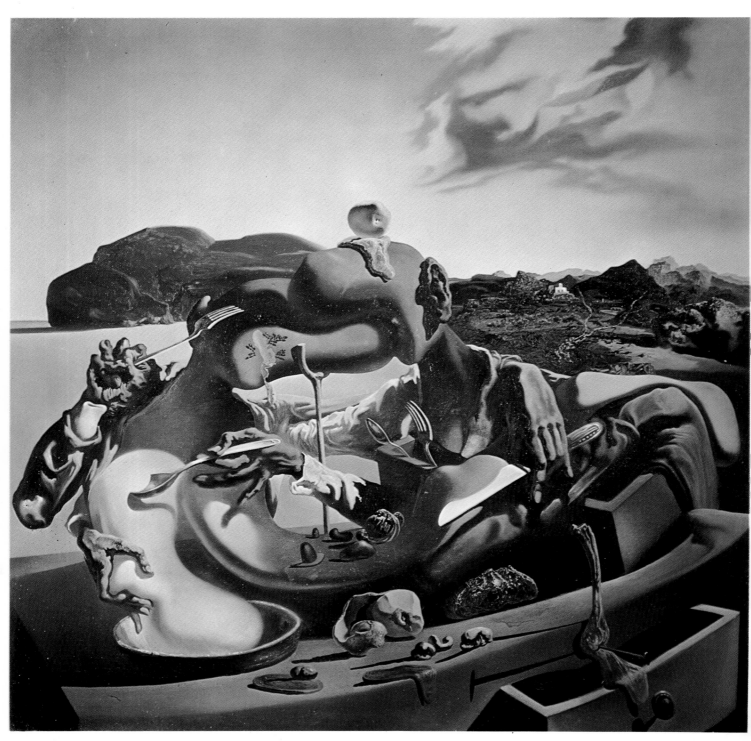

Plate 35 **Autumn Cannibalism**

ugly'). It was nevertheless a discouraging period for Dali. The sale of his paintings following the Goeman's exhibition was not going well, which he blamed on 'the freemasonry of modern art'. Goemans had gone into bankruptcy owing him money. If the public would not buy his works, perhaps they would buy his inventions. Each day Gala would walk the streets of Paris with a portfolio of drawings for such items as transparent mannequins for shop windows, their bodies filled with water and live goldfish, bakelite furniture shaped to fit the body contours, shoes with springs to augment the pleasure of walking, artificial fingernails made of tiny reducing mirrors in which one saw oneself, dresses with false insets and anatomical padding to titillate man's erotic fantasies. Rejected as uncommercial at the time, many were to make their appearance as a result of his influence, for which he received no credit.

Dali was to carry out many Surrealist objects for the English collector, Edward James, whom he called 'the humming-bird poet'. The Mae West sofa, made in the shape of her lips and taken from the portrait he made of her, the famous lobster telephone and, in James's country house in Sussex, the white grand piano rising from the centre of a pond with jets of water spouting from the keyboard.

As early as 1914 Marcel Duchamp[1] has chosen 'ready-mades' and 'aided ready-mades' which could be considered the first Surrealist objects. In 1924 André Breton had suggested the making of certain objects which one only sees in dreams. In the following years Surrealism was to draw attention to various categories of objects: the found object, interpreted object, phantom object, poem object and the object functioning symbolically, invented by Dali, which were based on phantasmagoria and representations produced by unconscious acts. These objects were intended to procure by indirect means a particular sexual emotion and, by calling on Dali's ultra-confusing activity rising out of the obsessing idea, led to the creation of such objects as *Retrospective Bust of a Woman Devoured by Ants*, *The Aphrodisiac Jacket*, to which fifty wine glasses filled with crème de menthe and a dead fly had been attached, and *Atmospheric Chair*, with a seat composed of bars of chocolate. On a more ambitious level were the two hundred live, edible snails which crawl over a semi-nude figure in an ivy-wreathed taxi.

Dali's shoe fetish goes back to his adolescence and appears in many paintings and objects. Schiaparelli created a hat in the form of a shoe based on an idea by him. It is an object 'most charged with realistic virtues as opposed to musical objects which I have always tried to represent as demolished, crushed, soft-cellos of rotten meat ...'

The Surrealist object, Dali maintained, discredited completely the dream period of Surrealism, and the meaningless writing dictated by the unconscious. He saw the object as a new reality, useless from a practical point of view but 'created wholly for the purpose of materialising in a fetishistic way, with the maximum of tangible reality, ideas and fantasies having a delirious character'. People would no longer

Plate 35
Autumn Cannibalism
1936–37
Oil on canvas
$31\frac{1}{2} \times 31\frac{1}{2}$ in (80 × 80 cm)
Edward James Foundation (on loan to the Tate Gallery, London)

One of Dali's most remarkable works and an astonishing triumph of imagination. Food has always been one of Dali's obsessions: 'Cooking is very close to painting,' he once said. 'When you are making a dish you add a little of this and a little of that ... it's like mixing paints.' In this painting of two beings in the act of devouring each other appear a number of familiar Dalian images—crutches, bread, ants as well as the instruments of mutilation.

[1]Although the marginal role of Marcel Duchamp in Surrealism is outside the scope of this book, his contribution to the movement had a certain validity for a time, in particular the anti-art objects distinguished by their banality. It was, however, his obsessive need to supply written confirmation of his philosophical speculations which was later on to bring him to the attention of the abstract artists of the 'establishment' modern school, many of whom now live off his projects and utterances.

Plate 36
Metamorphosis of Narcissus
1936–37
Oil on canvas
20 × 30 in (50.8 × 76.3 cm)
Edward James Foundation (on
loan to the Tate Gallery, London)

Dali explained this painting to
Freud, when they met in London
in 1938, prompting Freud to re-
mark: 'I have never seen a more
complete example of a Spaniard.
What a fanatic!' The work was
literally illustrated by a poem Dali
wrote at the same time, on the
theme of the death and fossilisation
of Narcissus.

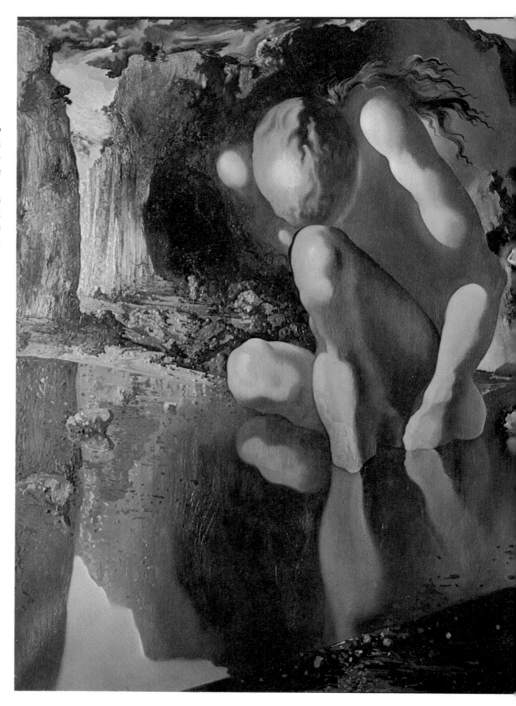

face the limitations of only talking about their manias and phobias,
'but could now touch them, manipulate and operate them with their
own hands'.

He also planned a number of bread objects. 'Not,' he maintained,
'precisely intended for the succour and sustenance of large families.
My bread was a ferociously anti-humanitarian bread, it was the
bread of the revenge of imaginative luxury on the utilitarianism of the
rational practical world ...' It was to be aristocratic, paranoiac,
paralysing and phenomenal. One idea in true Dali style was to bake a
loaf fifteen metres long, which was to be placed, wrapped in newspaper, in the gardens of the Palais Royal. The public reaction and
speculation was then to be reported in detail. Next day a loaf twenty

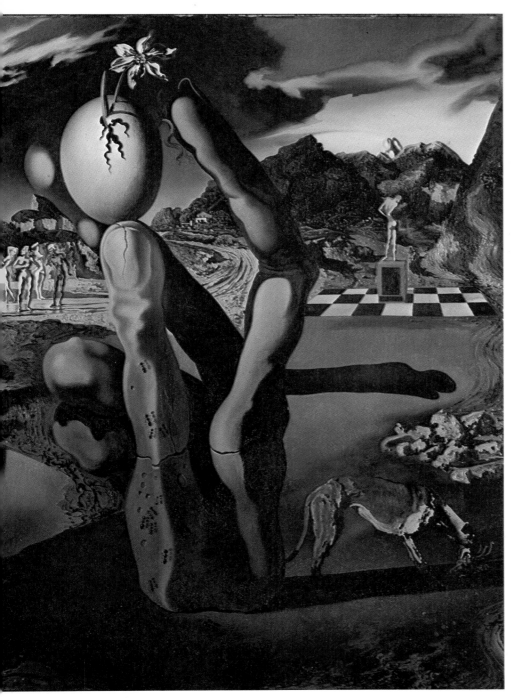

Plate 37 *overleaf*
Sleep
1937
Oil on canvas
20 × 30¾ in (50.8 × 78.2 cm)
New Trebizond Foundation

Dali saw sleep as a monster supported by crutches.

metres long would be found in the court of Versailles, to be followed by thirty-metre loaves appearing simultaneously in the public squares of various capitals of Europe.

For the first New York World's Fair in 1939 Dali's *Dream of Venus* involved seventeen live mermaids in a water-filled tank : some milked an underwater cow, others played pianos or were answering telephones. Obeying only the laws of chance or of psychic necessity, such objects established a canon of the unexpected, lending coherence to a dream world which identified itself with a new exciting and poetic experience. They demonstrated the validity of Lautréamont's contention that poetry can be made by all.

Dali's ceaseless intervention into all aspects of Surrealist activity—

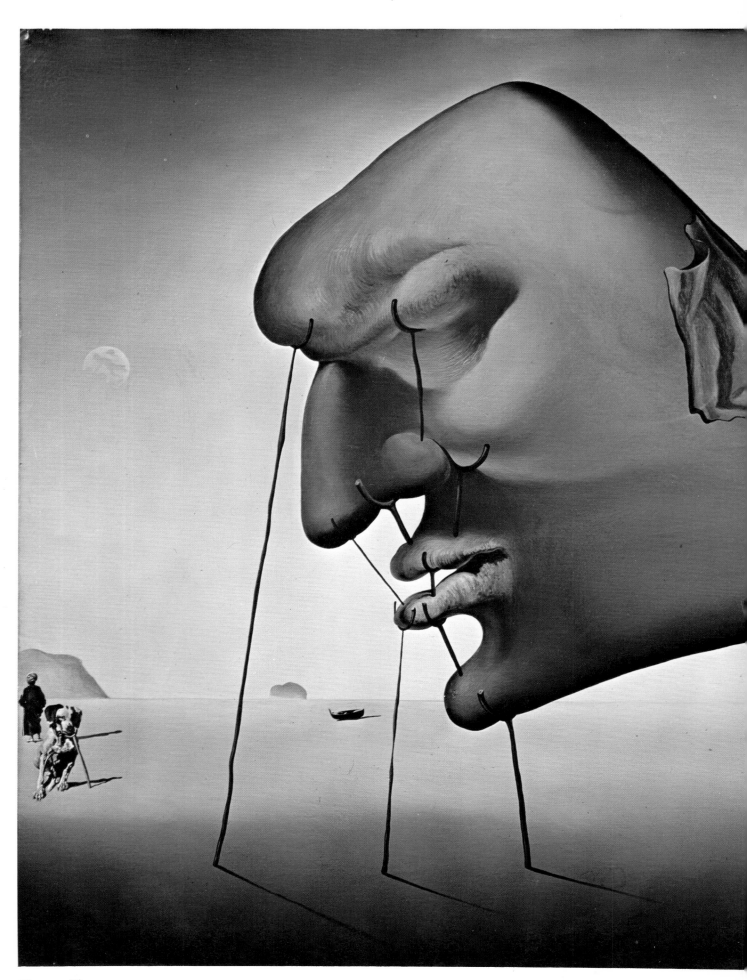

Plate 37 **Sleep**

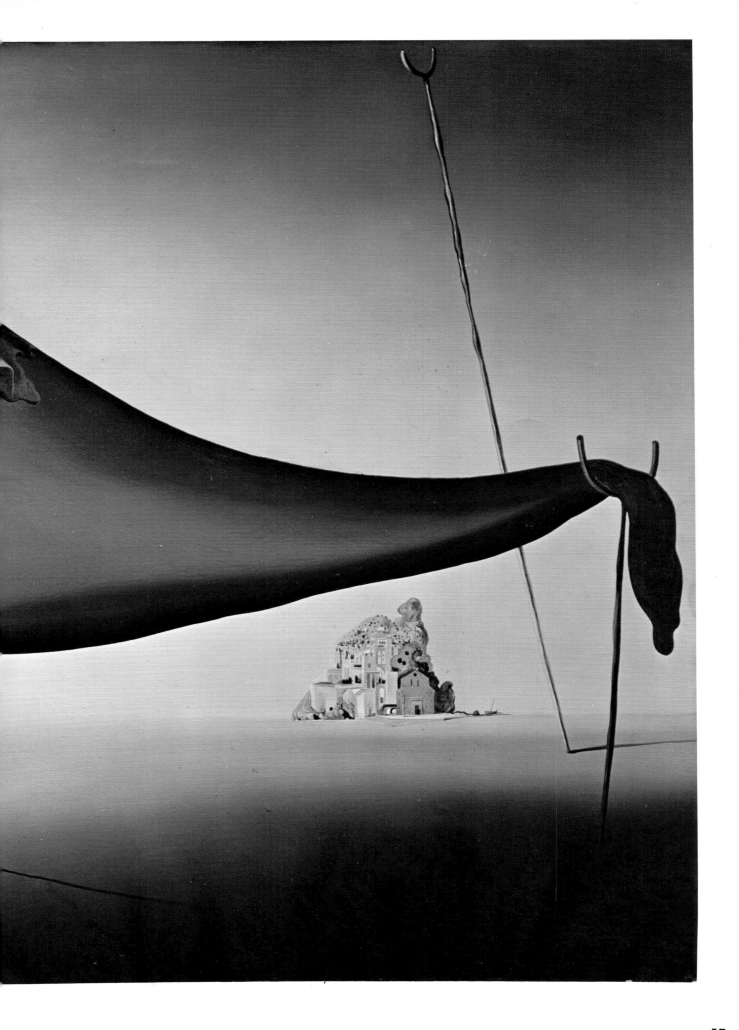

Plate 38
Hieronymus Bosch
The Garden of Earthly Delights
Right-hand panel
Oil on wood
The Prado, Madrid

There have been many attempts to
see Dali as the Hieronymus Bosch
of our time, an error he has cor-
rected in the following statement:
'Bosch's monsters are the product
of fog-shrouded Nordic forests and
the awful indigestion of the Middle
Ages. The results are symbolic
characters, and satire took advan-
tage of that gigantic diarrhoea. It's
a universe I'm not interested in. In
fact it's the exact opposite of
monsters who are born in a different
way and who, on the contrary, issue
from the overplus of Mediterranean
light.'

Plate 39
Inventions of the Monsters
1937
Oil on canvas
$20\frac{1}{8} \times 30\frac{7}{8}$ in (51 × 78.5 cm)
The Joseph Winterbotham
Collection, Art Institute of
Chicago

Dali's interest in the Italian masters
and in established aesthetic values
began to have an impact on his
work. To the 'great Realists', like
Velásquez and Vermeer of Delft, he
now added Leonardo, as in the
foreground figure, recognisable as
Leonardo's Madonna. The two
figures seated alongside are portraits of the artist and Gala.

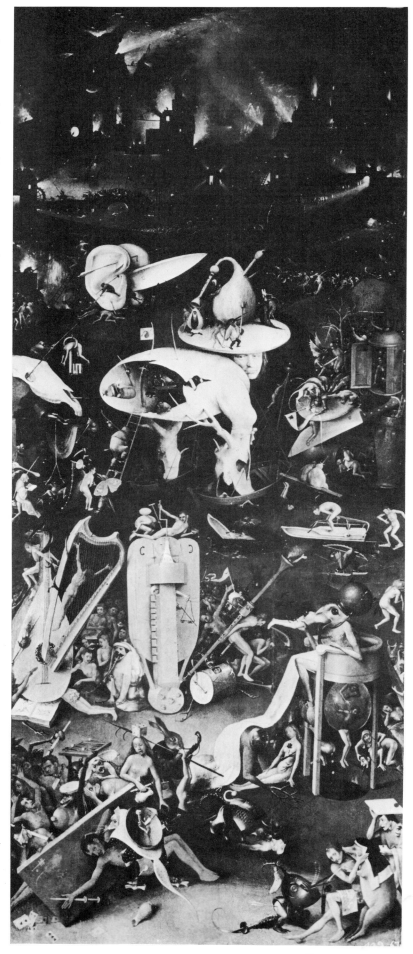

his critical writing, painting, his objects and poetry – were all essential contributions to the vitality of the movement. His obsession with all aspects of visual phenomena and his fascination with giving life to the inanimate and seeking out hidden biological meanings have formed the theses for his ideological inspiration, 'a Renaissance man converted to psychoanalysis', according to Sarane Alexandrian.[1]

Only in a few instances has Dali offered any explanation as to the meaning of his paintings. In *Conquest of the Irrational* he wrote: 'The fact that I myself, at the moment of painting, do not understand my own pictures does not mean that these pictures have no meaning; on the contrary, their meaning is so profound, complex, coherent and involuntary that it escapes the most simple analysis of logical intuition. To describe my pictures in everyday language, to explain them, it is necessary to submit them to special analyses, and preferably with the most ambitiously objective scientific rigour possible.' Then all explanation arises *a posteriori* once the picture already exists as a phenomenon.' The disquieting limp watches in *The Persistence of Memory* (plate 14) came into being as a result of eating Camembert cheese, with its particular softness. 'You may be sure that the famous soft watches are nothing else than the tender, extravagant, solitary, paranoiac-critical Camembert of time and space.' Marcel Jean[2] gives a more illuminating explanation. 'The word *montre* (watch) is a word-image with a double meaning: in French, it is the imperative

[1] *Surrealist Art,* Thames & Hudson, London, 1970.

[2] *The History of Surrealist Painting,* Editions de Seuil, Paris, 1959.

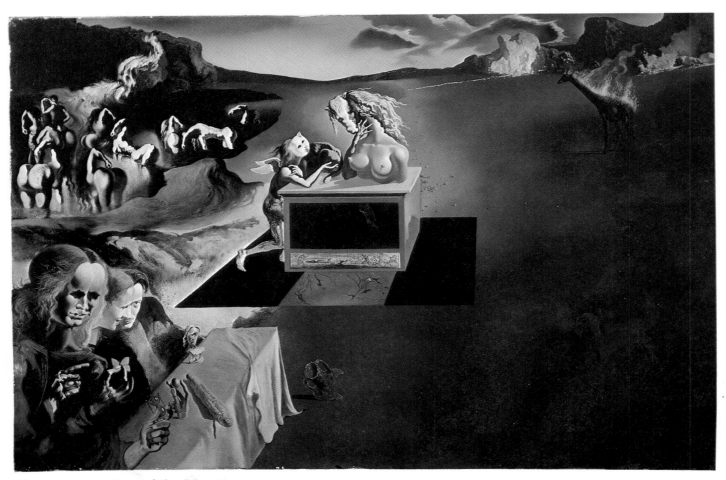

Plate 39 **Inventions of the Monsters**

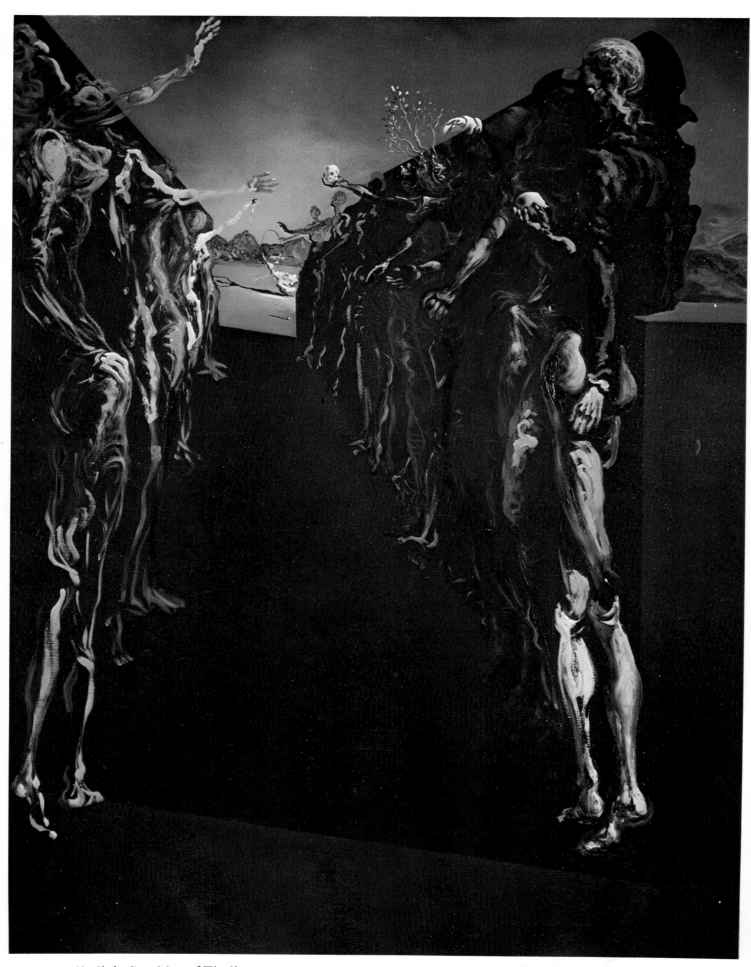

Plate 40 **Palladio's Corridor of Thalia**

of the verb *montrer* (to show) and the name of the apparatus *montrant* (showing) the time. But there is a very common childhood experience: the doctor asks the sick child to *montrer sa langue* (show his tongue), which obviously is soft. The child, we may say, *la montre molle* (shows it soft, with the double sense that in French this phrase can also mean 'the soft watch'). The irrational and even anguished nature of this act for the child, in view of the circumstances, could certainly constitute an experience capable of leaving profound impressions in the psyche. Here, then, is a most concrete origin for the image of the soft watches, an origin founded in an authentic childhood memory, which seems to be confirmed by the titles of the picture ...' Bought by the American gallery owner Julien Levy, it was sold and resold until it was finally hung in the Museum of Modern Art, New York. It was to achieve such popular success that reproductions were used to attract custom to furniture and vegetable shops.

A few years later he was to paint *The Spectre of Sex Appeal* with his explanation 'of having predicted in 1928, at the height of the cult for functional and practical anatomy, in the midst of the most shocking scepticism, the imminence of the round and salivary muscles of Mae West, viscous and terrible with hidden biological meanings. Today I announce that all the new sexual allure of women will come from the possible utilisation of their capacities and resources as ghosts, that is to say, their possible dissociation, their charnel and luminous decomposition.' Now women with sex appeal would have detachable portions of their anatomy, which they could hand round for admiration. It seems unlikely that this painting is the result of hypnotic trance or hallucination so much as an attempt, in clear consciousness, to realise one of his inspired ideas. It is conceived in brilliant colours, because he wanted it to be 'more beautiful and terrifying than the white truffle of death: a rainbow'. The image of the crutches that support the spectre, and appear in many later paintings, began when he was a child staying with Señor Pitchot. Dali sees the crutch fetish in two ways: firstly sociologically, for a wealthy but weak society in need of support; secondly he sees in the shape of the crutch the significance of life and death – a support for his imagined feeling of inadequacy. The monstrous bodiless head of *Sleep* (plate 37) is propped up with innumerable crutches, not only raising it off the ground but holding its features – lips, nose and eyes. He speaks of them as 'wooden supports derived from Cartesian philosophy. Generally used as a support for the tenderness of soft structure.'

By 1934 Dali had directed his attention to what he was to call 'instant-aneous' figures, possibly inspired by the particular effect of sunlight that is found on the beach at Rosas, situated a few miles from Figueras, although in his memoirs he talks of painting a few apparently very normal paintings, 'inspired by the congealed and minute enigma of certain snapshots, to which I added a Dalinian touch of Meissonier ...' The ostensible subject matter could certainly have been released

Plate 40
Palladio's Corridor of Thalia
1937
Oil on canvas
$46\frac{1}{4} \times 35\frac{5}{8}$ in (117.5×90.5 cm)
Edward James Foundation

Palladio's stage sets for the Teatro Olimpico in Vicenza, with their dramatic use of perspective, have been transformed by Dali into human forms. He was to paint another variation on the theme, *Palladio's Corridor of Dramatic Surprise*, in 1938. Since the animate and the inanimate are indistinguishable according to his 'paranoiac' ability, Dali sees no reason why such inanimate objects as chests, telephones and in this case architecture should not assume living forms.

61

Plate 41
Giuseppe Arcimboldo
Summer
1563
Kunstistorisches Museum, Vienna

The ambiguous double-image was used by many artists of the 16th and 17th centuries. It was to play an important part in Dali's iconography, and through his 'paranoiac-critical method' he was able to recognise hidden meanings in the most unlikely subjects.

Plate 42
Spain
1938
Oil on canvas
36 × 23⅝ in (91.5 × 60 cm)
New Trebizond Foundation

Dali's use of the multiple image is a genuine *tour de force*. The equestrian battle in the distance, influenced by Leonardo, is so arranged as to form the face of the woman leaning on the chest in the foreground.

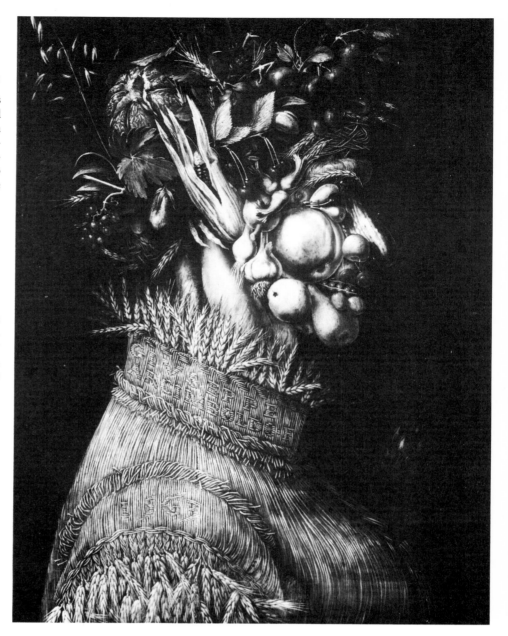

by seeing old snapshots of his childhood and memories of being with his nurse on the beach. These figures are, possibly, phantoms, sublimated versions, as Freud has said, of 'the nocturnal visitors attired in nightdresses, who awoke the child to put him on the chamberpot so that he should not wet the bed, or who lifted the bedclothes in order to see how he held his hands in sleep'. An important feature in the works of this period is the stereoscopic effect produced by these figures against a background, as well as the complete lack of distortion in the treatment. Also discernible is a distinct move towards aesthetic values. *Paranoiac-Astral Image*, *Apparition on the Beach at Rosas*, as well as *Noon*, although free of his usual mannerisms and fetishistic devices, achieve an apparitional effect and project a condition of apprehension that is recognised in hallucinations or in dreams. They capture a haunting premonition of a secret activity that lies midway between actual reality and the magic realm of unconscious desires.

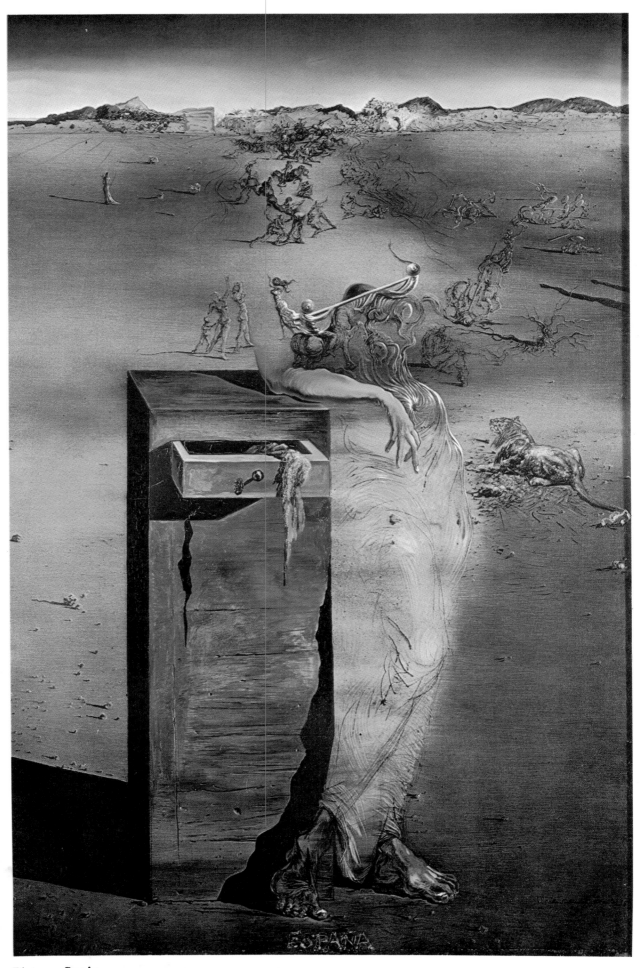

Plate 42 **Spain**

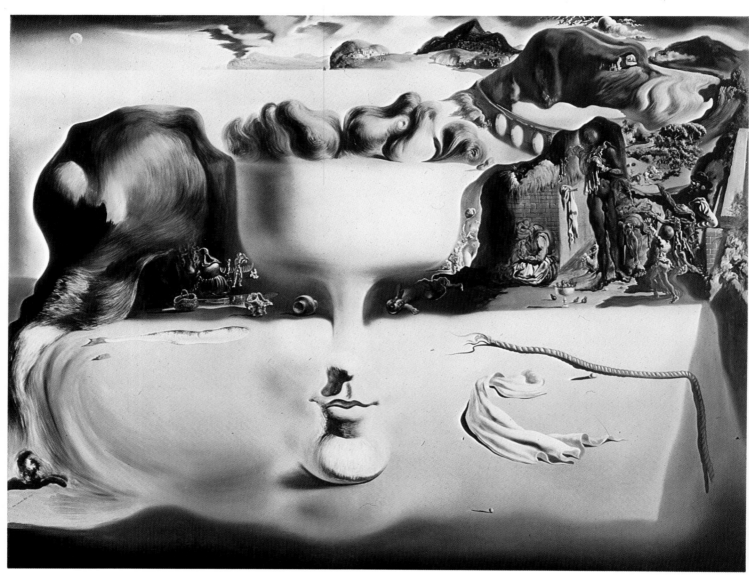

Plate 43 **Apparition of a Face and Fruit-dish on a Beach**

Not unrelated to the Rosas series of paintings is one of his most strikingly poetic works, *The Phantom Cart* (plate 20), in which we see that the back of the two figures seated in the cart are really part of the buildings in the distant town. By some strange alchemy, the cart has already reached its destination while it is still some way off.

On the occasion of the Surrealist exhibition at the Galerie Colle in 1933, Dali had proposed a catalogue preface praising the art of Meissonier, a popular academic of the last century, for his 'irrational exactness'. Opposition among the Surrealists was unanimous. They saw little purpose in recognising such a painter as a model of Surrealism. More disquieting was Dali's interest in Nazism and Hitler's rise to power in Germany.[1] A 'Hitlerian nurse' had made its appearance in certain works, while in *The Enigma of William Tell* (plate 23) a portrait of Lenin appeared, without any trousers and with an extended buttock supported by a crutch. It was to show a very different tribute from *Six Apparitions of Lenin on a Piano* (plate 13), painted in the previous year. *Six Apparitions*, for all its complex imagery, could be taken as a sign of Dali's sympathy with Surrealism's political leanings. Understandably, though, such works by the Surrealists were not likely to meet with the Communists' approval, who believed in a Social Realist art, and this soon led to a break between the groups, with the formation of an 'Association of Revolutionary Writers and Artists' by the Surrealists, which Dali refused to join.

In the political climate of the time, with Surrealism taking a more positive attitude against the forces of capitalism, changing *La Revolution Surrealiste* to *Le Surrealisme au Service de la Revolution* ('Surrealism in the Service of the Revolution'), Dali's uneasy relationship with the movement, following the success of his first exhibition in New York at the Julien Levy Gallery, which had identified him as the only authentic voice of Surrealism, along with his growing interest in the aristocracy, monarchy and Catholicism, led to a confrontation with the Surrealists at a meeting in André Breton's house.

Accounts vary on what took place at this meeting. Some say he was officially expelled, others that he was being censured for the wilder eccentricities. Dali turned up with a thermometer in his mouth, pretending to have 'flu. As the discussion became more heated, he kept checking his temperature, and with each attack on him proceeded to take off one of the numerous shirts he was wearing until, naked to the waist, he threw himself at Breton's feet. Dali's defence was that his obsession with Hitler was purely paranoid and apolitical, and he would probably be one of the first to be done away with as a degenerate, if Europe was conquered. Not all the Surrealists were unanimous in their opposition, and Dali succeeded so well in creating an atmosphere of confusion and hysteria that the affair eventually petered out. Although Dali no longer attended the meetings, he was still invited to contribute to the group's exhibitions, including the controversial portrait of Lenin, which was shown at the Galerie Bonjean in 1934.

It was nevertheless the first sign, which Breton had already

Plate 43
Apparition of Face and Fruit-dish on a Beach
1938
Oil on canvas
45 × 57½ in (114 × 146 cm)
E. G. and M. C. Sumner Collection, Wadsworth Atheneum, Hartford (Connecticut)

The multiple image is revealed in a sequence of subjects. The base of the dish is also the back view of his nurse of the Rosas series, which in turn also becomes a face. The dog's head is part of the beach, its back composed of fruit. Dali wrote: 'The double image may be extended, continuing the paranoiac advance, and then the presence of another dominant idea is enough to make a third image appear, and so on, until there is a number of images limited only by the mind's degree of paranoiac capacity.'

[1] Although Dali kept silent during the Spanish civil war, his sympathy was with Franco. Since the last war he has again expressed his admiration for Hitler.

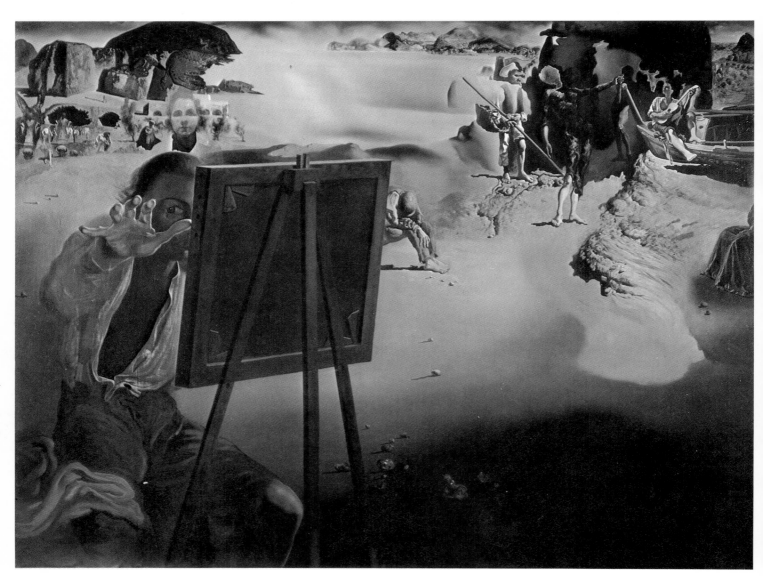

Plate 44 **Impressions of Africa**

detected when he wrote the introduction to Dali's first Paris exhibition. But 'the sound of Dali's admirable voice' was to last only a few more years. In the meanwhile he continued to enrich the movement with his researches.

Between 1933 and 1936, Dali applied his mental and plastic resources to a number of inspirational sources, as well as making literary contributions to *Minotaure*, and to *Cahiers d'Art* for which he wrote an article on Surrealist objects. He began to explore various skeletal and cephalic deformations, in which figures take on grotesquely deformed growths. *Average Atmospherocephalic Bureaucrat in the Act of Milking a Cranial Harp, Myself at the Age of Ten when I was the Grasshopper Child*, as well as *Meditation on the Harp*, are typical examples of his clinical imagination, made all the more disturbing because of our knowledge that certain people are victims of such disfigurations.

It was not difficult to see in the slightly ridiculous figure, without trousers, in the act of milking the soft monstrosity, a clearly masturbatory image, while *Meditation on the Harp* draws on the devout image of the man in Millet's *Angelus* being embraced by a voluptuous nude as he hides an erection behind his hat.

In only one instance, inspired by these deformations, *Soft Construction with Boiled Beans: Premonition of Civil War*, which was painted in 1936, did Dali offer some explanation of his thoughts: 'I showed a vast human body breaking out into monstrous excrescences of arms and legs tearing at one another in a delirium of auto-strangulation. As a background to this architecture of frenzied flesh devoured by a narcissistic and biological cataclysm, I painted a geological landscape, that had been uselessly revolutionised for thousands of years, congealed in its "normal course". The soft structure of that great mass of flesh in civil war I embellished with a few boiled beans, for one could not imagine swallowing all that unconscious meat without the presence (however uninspiring) of some mealy and melancholy vegetable.'

Another approximation of his obsession with elongated growths supported by a crutch is *The Javanese Mannequin*, with its delicately wrought skeletal body.

Among the figures of rhetoric, there is one known as catachresis, by which the imagination supplies a known word to partially describe a new object—for instance, we speak of the foot of a table, or the arm of a windmill, taking from two different objects the means to create a third one. The Oxford *Shorter English Dictionary* gives as an example, 'Lakes by the figure catachresis called seas'. Used in a visual sense, they could be described as lyrical relations, when the outline of a hill and a reclining nude are interchangeable. Less familiar among Dali's works is a small painting entitled *Skull with its Lyrical Appendage Leaning on a Night Table which should have the Temperature of a Cardinal's Nest* (plate 26), showing a liquefying piano, its black and white keyboard stretched in such a manner that the keys metamorphose into the teeth of an adjoining skull. In a more restrained

Plate 44
Impressions of Africa
1938
Oil on canvas
36 × 46¼ in (91.5 × 117.5 cm)
Edward James Foundation (on loan to the Tate Gallery, London)

'Africa accounts for something in my work, since without having been there I remember so much about it!'

Dali had certainly read Raymond Roussel's *Impressions of Africa*, which are entirely imaginary, and which he said had been inspired by some opera glasses with the bazaar of Cairo painted on one lens and the bazaar of Luxor on the other.

The brushwork shows the influence of Velásquez. The figure at the easel is a self-portrait and a number of double images are evident in the background.

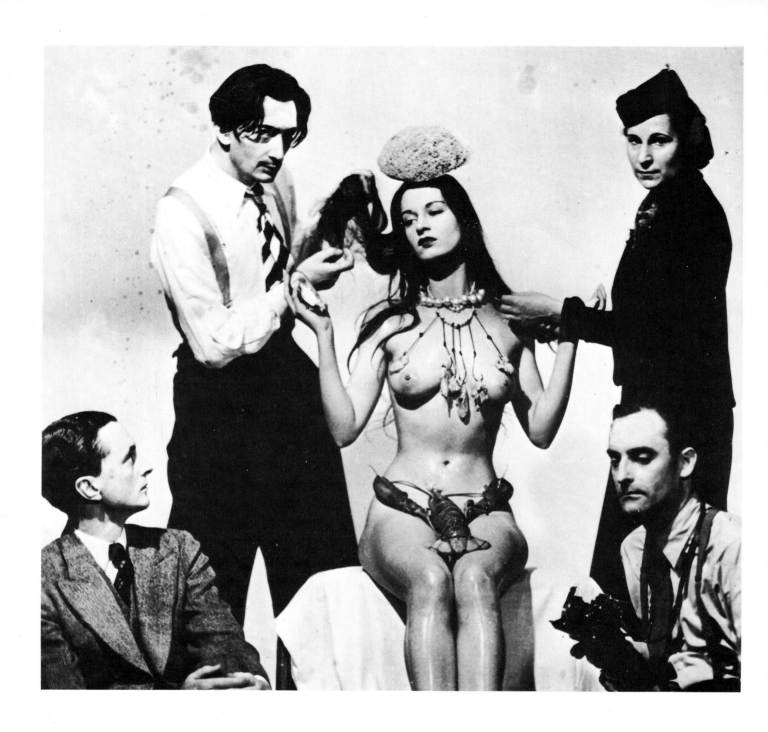

Plate 45
Dali and Gala arranging a living mannequin for the New York World Fair in 1939.

vein is *Nostalgic Echo* in which the outline of the young girl skipping is repeated in the shape of the bell in the tower and in the keyhole in the chest, while the shape of the wall in the foreground is repeated in the bell tower itself. Dali's debt to de Chirico is again recognisable in the girl skipping and the shadow of an unseen presence. It is a direct allusion to the most marvellous of de Chirico's paintings, *The Mystery and Melancholy of a Street*. The reference is further strengthened by its stillness, the feeling that time itself is frozen, with everything bathed in a strange melancholy.

It was not until 1931 that the first important exhibition of Surrealism was to take place outside of France. An American show was quickly followed by Dali's one-man exhibition in Barcelona. Then E. L. T. Mesens initiated another group show in Brussels in

1934. From then onwards Surrealist exhibitions became frequent—Copenhagen, Prague, Tokyo, Tenerife, Holland—and groups were formed in some fifteen countries. In June 1936 a large international exhibition was opened in the New Burlington Galleries, London. Organised by Roland Penrose, with the collaboration of the French and Belgian groups, it brought together pictures, objects, drawings, collages, sculptures, African and American primitive objects as well as children's drawings. Dali was represented by twelve works, including the *Retrospective Bust of a Woman* and *Aphrodisiac Jacket*.

During the opening, a young woman wandered through the gallery dressed in a white gown, her head and face completely covered with roses on which rested live ladybirds. She wore long black surgical gloves and carried a model human leg in one hand and a raw pork chop in the other.[1] The exhibition was opened by André Breton, dressed in green, smoking a green pipe, accompanied by his wife with long green hair. During the exhibition Dali was to give a lecture in a diving suit, which had been rented by Lord Berners for the occasion. When he was asked to specify the depth of the descent, he replied that Mr Dali was going to descend to the unconscious. In that case, the suppliers assured him, they would replace the usual helmet with a special one. Dali appeared in the suit, decorated with plasticine hands, a radiator cap on top of the helmet, a dagger in the belt and holding

Plate 46
Slave Market with Disappearing Bust of Voltaire
1940
Oil on canvas
$18\frac{1}{4} \times 25\frac{3}{4}$ in (46.3×65.5 cm)
Collection of Mr and Mrs
A. Reynolds Morse, Salvador Dali Museum, Cleveland (Ohio)

Voltaire's face appears in a number of works. Here it will be recognised in the two figures dressed in black, whose faces go to form the eyes of Voltaire. The area of sky seen through the irregular arch behind them forms the head.

[1] In Marcel Jean's *History of Surrealist Painting*, she is shown in Trafalgar Square among the pigeons.

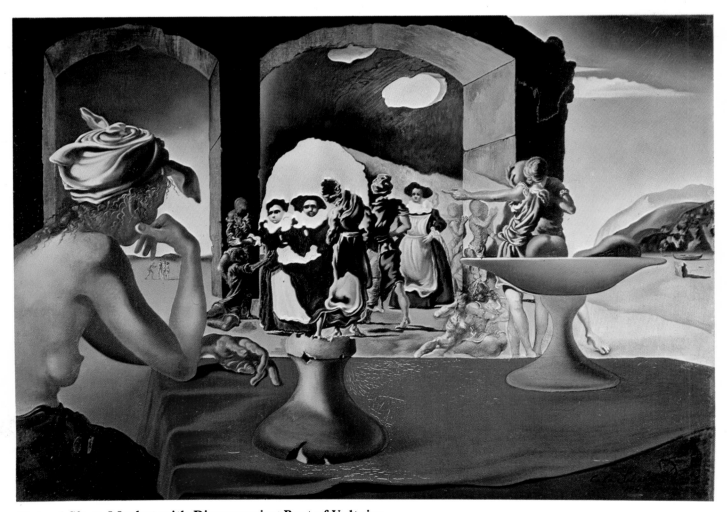

Plate 46 **Slave Market with Disappearing Bust of Voltaire**

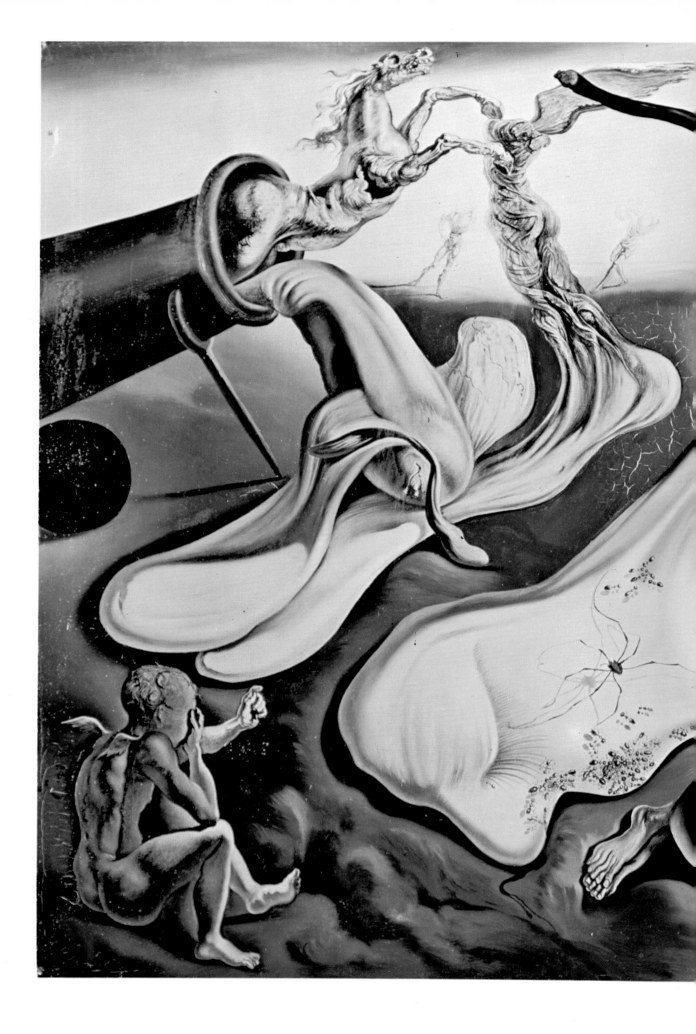

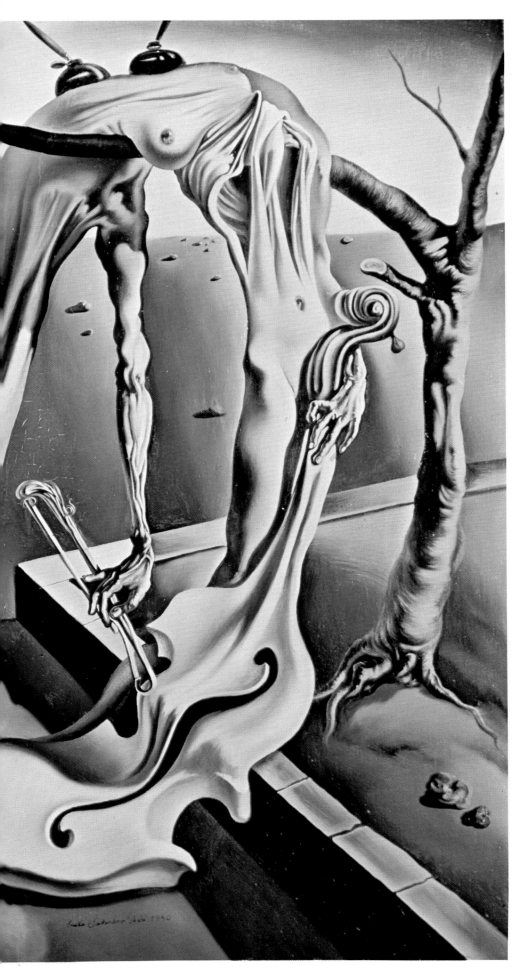

Plate 47
Daddy Long Legs–Hope
1940
Oil on canvas
16 × 20 in (40.5 × 50.8 cm)
Private collection

**Geopoliticus Child Watching
the Birth of the New Man**
1943
Oil on canvas
18 × 20½ in (45.7 × 52 cm)
Collection of Mr and Mrs
A. Reynolds Morse, Salvador
Dali Museum, Cleveland (Ohio)

Dali's decision to become classical
and to 'paint pictures uniquely
consecrated to the architecture of
the Renaissance and the Special
Sciences' was made in 1941, and a
growing academicism in his technique became noticeable.

two Russian wolfhounds on leads. After trying to deliver his lecture,
quite inaudibly from inside the helmet, Dali, dripping with perspi-
ration and nearly suffocating from lack of air, gestured wildly to have
the helmet removed, only to discover that the mechanic had locked
the bolts so securely that no one could remove it.

The end of this year saw a number of works, among which was the
remarkable painting *Autumn Cannibalism* (plate 35), in which a
liquefying figure spreads itself over a chest, as it eats itself with a
knife and fork. One of Dali's great contributions was to show the
chaotic background to the work of art; mitigated by aesthetic
control his pictures would not be what they are, and while much of
his work might be considered external documentation, *Autumn
Cannibalism* is a triumph of imagination. It is as though he has
translated all the desires of humanity into flesh and not as usual into
form.

It was two years later, in London, that Dali realised one of his
greatest ambitions, to meet Sigmund Freud, made possible with the
help of Stefan Zweig. While crossing the yard on the day of the
meeting, Dali reported, 'I saw a bicycle leaning against the wall, and
on the saddle, attached by a string, was a red rubber hot-water bottle,
which looked full of water and on the back of the hot-water bottle
walked a snail.'[1]

Freud, then seriously ill, is reported to have made only two
remarks: 'In classic paintings, I look for the sub-conscious–in a
Surrealist painting, for the conscious.' As his guests left, he turned to
Zweig, saying: 'I have never seen a more complete example of a
Spaniard. What a fanatic.' Dali was later to claim that Freud's pro-
nouncement on Surrealist painting was a death sentence for the
doctrine. From now on it was to be not experimentation but tradition,
not revolution but renaissance.

Dali's patron, Edward James, bought many of his works during
that period, and he was a frequent guest at James's house. At that
time his English was practically non-existent, which could account for
the misunderstanding that arose upon hearing someone talk of 'a
chest of drawers'. Interpreting this quite literally, Dali in *Anthropo-
morphic Cabinet* as well as a number of drawings, was to show a
reclining woman out of whose chest appeared numerous half-open
drawers. The idea could have been supplemented by an awareness
of the 17th-century drawings of Bracelli, showing the human figure
constructed of such items as boxes, tennis rackets and bell towers.

Few artists have shown their contempt for the machine so strongly
as Dali. Contemporary industrial products are invariably treated with
savage disregard for their natural properties, either by transforming
them into living forms, or by reducing them to the fury of disintegration. The motor car which appears in a number of his works never
looks as though it will run, and in *Paranoiac-Critical Solitude* (plate
28) it has been excavated, fossil-like, from the rock. 'Machines are
doomed to crumble and rust,' he claimed. Mechanical brains like

[1] He had earlier discovered that Freud's
cranium was a snail–a spiral brain.

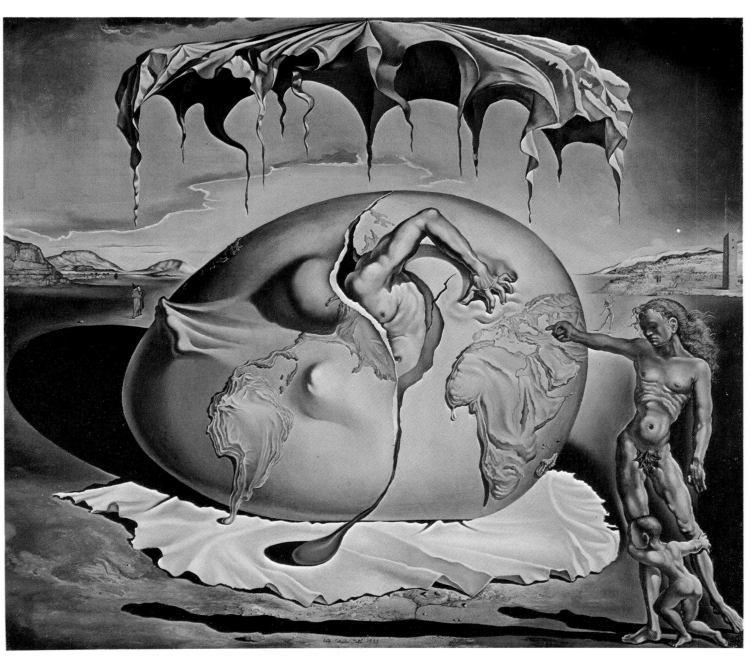

Plate 48 **Geopoliticus Child Watching the Birth of the New Man**

Plate 49
Apotheosis of Homer
1945
Oil on canvas
25¼ × 47 in (64 × 119 cm)
Staatsgalerie Moderner Kunst,
Munich

Dali has now become fascinated
with themes of Christianity as well
as discoveries in physics. About this
work he has merely said, 'Detailed
narration of the world of the blind'.
The work was to signify the end of
his Surrealist career.

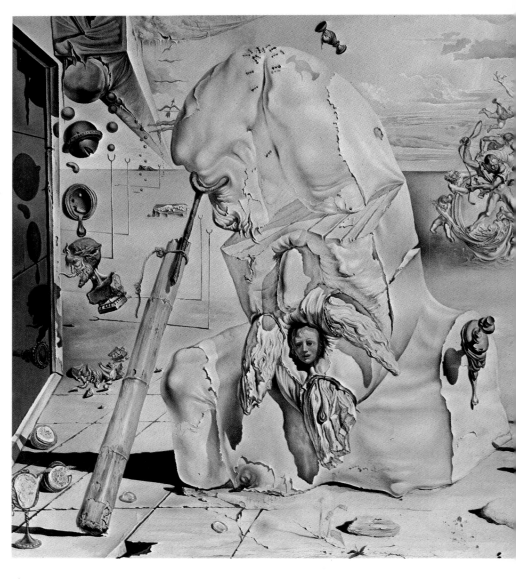

television kill imagination and the spirit of man. Why were people
so incapable of fantasy? Why, for instance, didn't manufacturers of
toilets hide a bomb in the flush, to detonate when politicians pulled
the cord? Why, when ordering lobster, didn't one get a cooked
telephone? Dali's hatred of mass-production led him to consider an
automobile in the absurd act of gestation, as in *Debris of an Automobile
giving Birth to a Blind Horse biting a Telephone.*

At some point during Dali's stay in England, he discovered the
paintings of the Pre-Raphaelite Brotherhood, in whose works he
found 'paranoiac' evidence. Their very literary subject matter and
highly elaborated symbolism, combined with an obsessional attention
to detail, were all qualities that appealed to Dali's own predilection.
When he wrote 'Le surréalisme spectral de l'éternal féminin pré-
raphaelite' ('The spectral surrealism of eternal Pre-Raphaelite
femininity'), it was not an attempt to justify the movement aesthe-
tically, but to explore the hidden meaning behind the outward
appearance. Breton had made clear the Surrealist's distrust of art
criticism. He saw it as 'a complete failure' because the critic describes

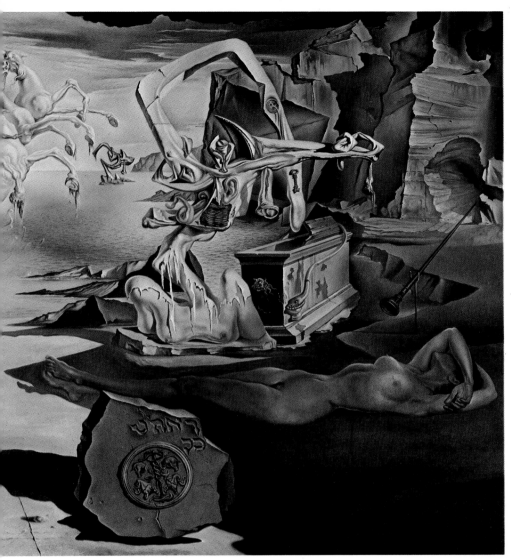

Plate 50 *overleaf*
The Madonna of Port Lligat
1950
Oil on canvas
56⅝ × 37¾ in (144 × 96 cm)
Lady Beaverbrook Collection,
Canada

Dali's preoccupation with a more conscious objectivity and also Roman Catholicism were the inspiration for the iconography of this work, about which he has said: 'The weaning of food-furniture made sacred: instead of a hole in my nurse's back, a tabernacle containing the divine bread open in the body of Jesus.'

Plate 51 *overleaf*
Christ of St John of the Cross
1951
Oil on canvas
90⅝ × 45⅝ in (230 × 103 cm)
Glasgow Art Gallery

the form rather than the content. The true value of any work was its ability, not to represent, but to prefigure. Breton suggested the search for a new beauty that would be acceptable to our time. 'Beauty will be convulsive,'[1] he insisted, and expressed his complete lack of interest in works of art that did not produce 'a state of physical disturbance characterised by the sensation of a wind brushing across my forehead and causing me to really shiver', a sensation he relates to erotic pleasure. Dali's paranoiac method, extended to his writings, contributed in no small measure to the revelatory nature of that which exists beneath the surface reality.

Unlike his other literary ventures into the significance of Millet's *Angelus*, the legend of William Tell and Art Nouveau, Dali's art showed no visual evidence of his meditations on the Pre-Raphaelites. Possibly he merely wished to illustrate his enthusiasm for all that ran counter to the prevailing fashion of the times and the appeal to 'the bad taste of the age' that Breton spoke of. It was not until 1944, in the painting *Tristan as Christ*, that Dali seems to have been partially inspired by Burne-Jones, in the detail of the jewelled breastplate,

[1] 'Beauty will be Convulsive', published in *What is Surrealism?*, translated by David Gascoyne, Faber & Faber, London, 1936.

75

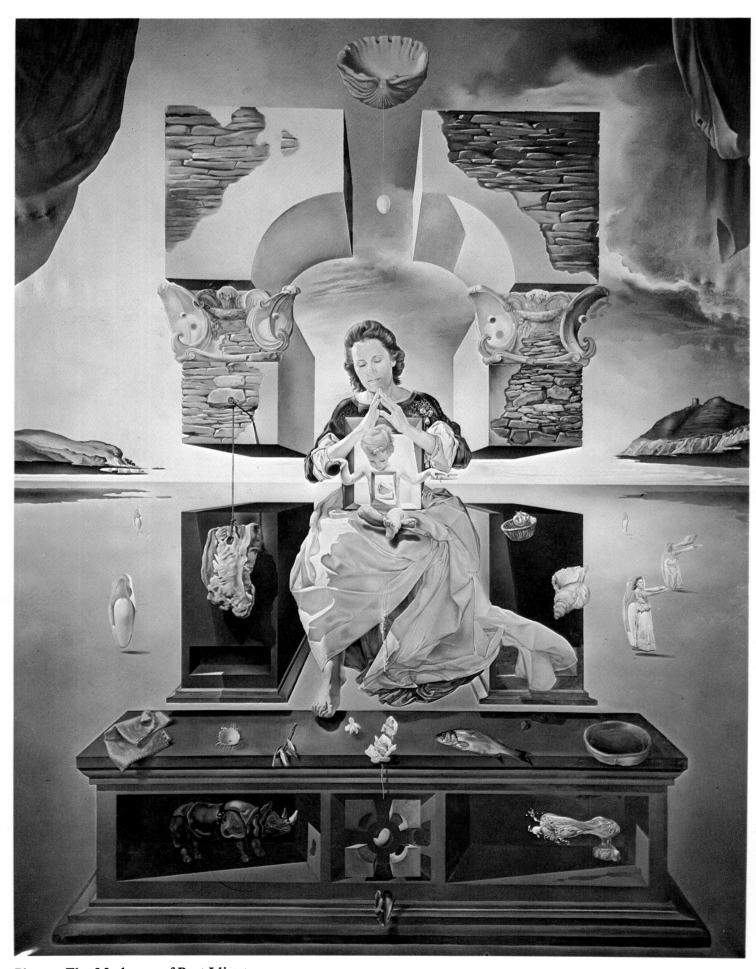

Plate 50 **The Madonna of Port Lligat**

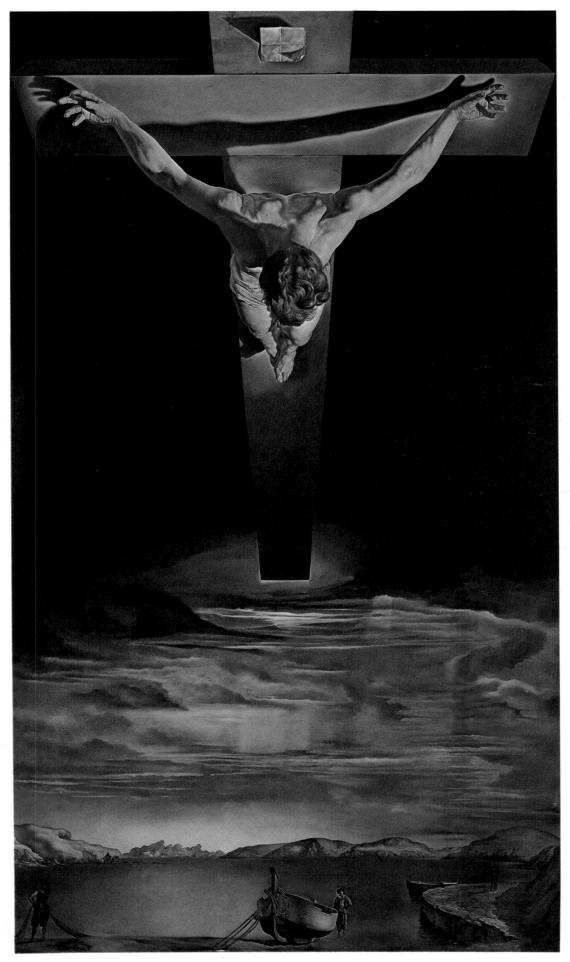

Plate 51 **Christ of St John of the Cross**

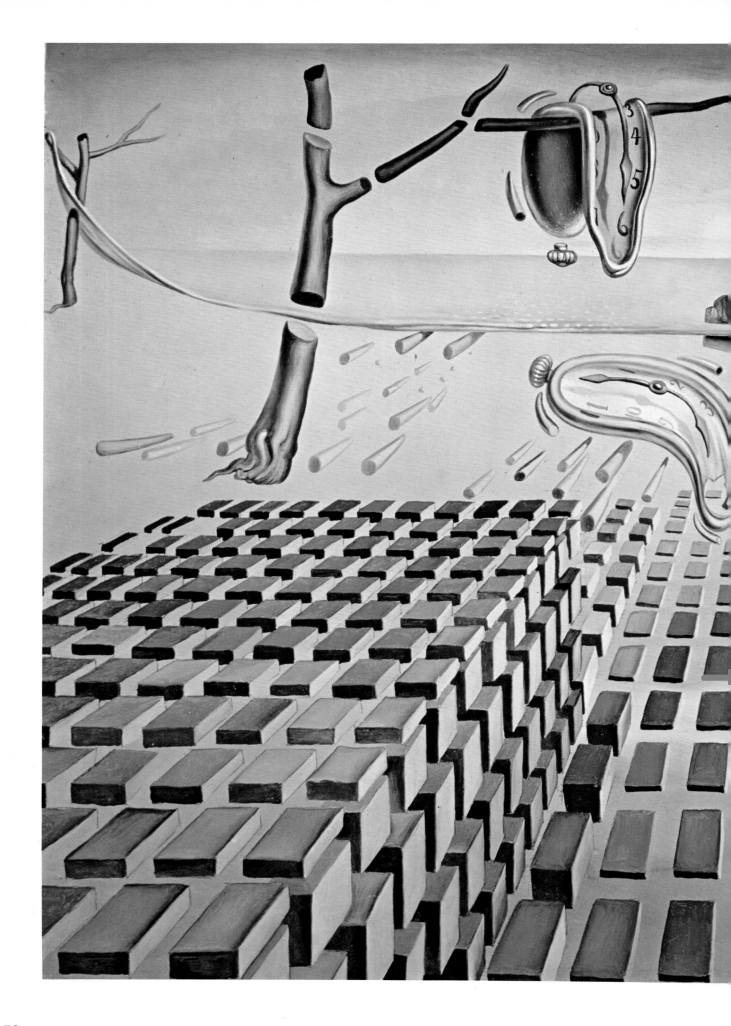

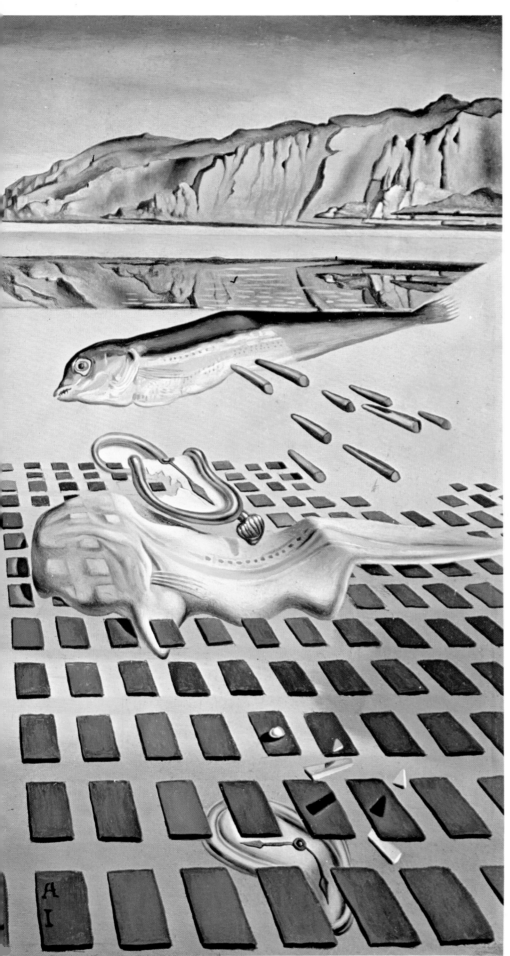

Plate 52
The Disintegration of the Persistence of Memory
1952–54
Oil on canvas
10 × 13 in (25.5 × 33 cm)
Collection of Mr and Mrs
A. Reynolds Morse, Salvador Dali
Museum, Cleveland (Ohio)

The full title of this work is *The Chromosome of a Highly Coloured Fish's Eye Starting the Harmonious Disintegration of the Persistence of Memory*. A number of compositional changes have been introduced into this work which is based on the 1931 *Persistence of Memory* (plate 14). The watch covered in ants has disappeared. The surface of the sea, sheet-like, hangs from the branch of a tree, and a fish now lies on what was a deserted beach.

'After twenty years of complete immobility,' said Dali, 'the soft watches disintegrate dynamically...'

Plate 53

Young Virgin Autosodomised by her own Chastity

1954
Oil on canvas
16 × 12 in (40.5 × 30.5 cm)
Selected by Hugh Hefner for the Playboy Collection.

About this painting Dali has said 'The horn of the rhinoceros, the former uniceros, is in fact the horn of the legendary unicorn, symbol of chastity. The young virgin can lean on it and play with it morally as was practised in the time of courtly love.'

the semi-transparent veil and preposterous pose of the figure that only revealed the dubious nature of his growing academicism.

Between 1937 and 1939, Dali made three visits to Italy. Rome, 'Catholic in essence and in substance', he found was being destroyed under Mussolini's modernisation, architecturally conceived 'by the brain of one of those lamentable organisers of international expositions'. He joined Edward James at Amalfi, where he found inspiration for his Wagnerian ballet and spent two months on *Impressions of Africa* (plate 44) in which the treatment owes more to Velásquez than to any Italian master. The Munich crisis of 1938 prompted a move to Monte Carlo and another painting, *The Enigma of Hitler*, based on dreams brought on by the events of Munich. This picture appeared to him 'to be charged with a prophetic value, as announcing the medieval period which was going to spread its shadow over Europe'. Chamberlain's umbrella appeared in this painting in a sinister aspect, identified with the bat, and 'affected me as extremely anguishing at the very time I was painting it ...'

In 1939 he made a second journey to America for his exhibition at the Julien Levy Gallery. New York, 'an immense Gothic Rocquefort cheese', was already familiar with this Paris Surrealist. His two previous exhibitions, lectures at the Museum of Modern Art, as well as the illustrations of the city made for the *American Weekly* in a four-page spread, left little doubt of his growing popularity with the American public. *Time* magazine put him on the cover, and Dali images soon appeared everywhere. The Fifth Avenue store of Bonwit-Teller invited him to make a window display. The theme was to be Night and Day. Night was symbolised by a bed with a canopy of a buffalo clutching a bloody pigeon in its mouth. The legs of the bed were the four feet of the animal. Black bedsheets were covered with burn marks, and a wax mannequin of the 1900 vintage, covered in dust and cobwebs, lay across the bed with her head resting on artificial live coals. Day showed another mannequin climbing into an ermine-lined bath filled with water, while a pair of wax arms held a mirror before her. Flowers grew out of the floor and surrounding furniture. The following day Dali discovered that the decor had been altered; his wax mannequins replaced by conventional ones and the bed removed. Furious at the treatment, Dali entered the display window and tried to upturn the bath of water in protest, only to slip and project the tub through the plate glass window into the watching crowd outside. Arrested by the police, he was brought before a night-court and given a suspended sentence.

No less disastrous from Dali's point of view was his sideshow for the New York World's Fair, to be called 'Dali's Dream of Venus'. He soon discovered that all the corporation wanted was his name, completely ignoring his ideas. Thoroughly disgusted, he sat down and wrote a manifesto, *Declaration of Independence of the Imagination and of the Rights of Man to his own Madness*. Before the 'Dream' was finished he left for France. The means Dali cynically used to publi-

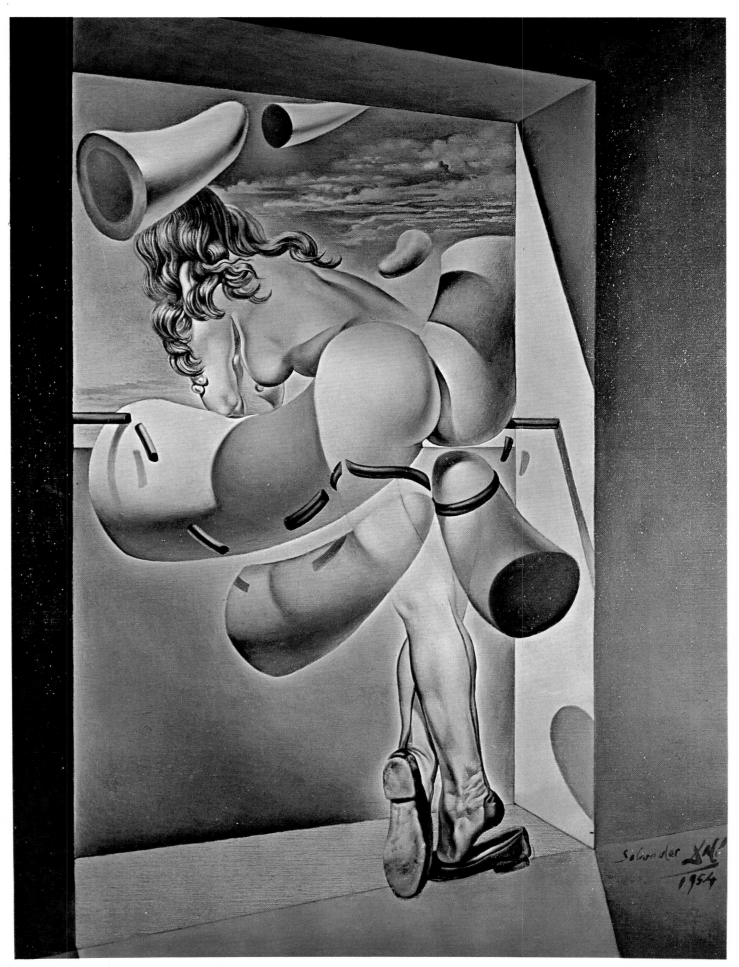

Plate 53 **Young Virgin Autosodomised by her own Chastity**

Plate 54
The Sacrament of the Last Supper
1955
Oil on canvas
$65\frac{3}{4} \times 105\frac{1}{2}$ in (167 × 268 cm)
Chester Dale Collection, National Gallery of Art, Washington (D.C.)

Dali based this work on the number 12: 12 hours of the day, 12 months of the year, 12 pentagons of the dodecahedron, 12 signs of the Zodiac, 12 Apostles around Christ.
'The Communion must be symmetrical,' he insisted.

cise himself, the endorsement of Franco in Spain and the growing academicism of his work had not passed unnoticed by the Surrealists, who rightly considered that he was bringing discredit to the ideas of Surrealism. This time the decision was unanimous: he was to be completely ignored by the movement. Dali had always insisted that he took Surrealism literally, neglected nothing to become the 'integral Surrealist' of which the logical outcome was his 'paranoiac-critical activity'. With equal determination he intended to 'become its leader as soon as possible', and to pass for the only authentic Surrealist. It was an attitude least calculated to identify him with a movement that had, since its inception, proclaimed a community of aims and had no wish to see Surrealism diminished by a wholehearted endorsement of his reactionary technique.

The advent of war brought a temporary truce to the Dali affair. After immense difficulties, some of the French Surrealists succeeded in reaching America. Man Ray and Nicholas Calas had arrived earlier and were soon joined by Tanguy, Masson, Matta, Duchamp, Seligmann and Breton. After moving to Spain, then Lisbon, Dali and Gala reached New York with the help of their friend, Caresse Crosby.[1] Recovering from their adventures at the country home of the Crosbys, Dali began writing his autobiography, widening his aesthetic interests and strengthening the ties with the Italian tradition. The Divine Proportion or, as Plato called it, the 'Golden Section' now received his attention, a principle he incorporated in the *Family of Marsupial Centaurs*, with its rigid diagonals dividing the composition into four equal triangles. Here Dali's hand is fully engaged by his conscious mind to achieve the Platonic ideal. It was to mark his reaction against the eloquence of his earlier works, in which revelation and discovery was the profound aim, and in which his masterly technique was used as a means and not as an end.

A return to classicism demanded a more conscious objectivity and a study of the pictorial science of the Renaissance. Geometry, mathematics, anatomy and perspective now received the same fanatical enthusiasm that earlier he had reserved for the interrogation of the unconscious as a springboard for inspiration. Both *Leda* and *Madonna and Child* are based on the Pythagorean pentagram, while the golden rectangle dominates *The Sacrament of the Last Supper* (plate 54). For Dali it meant 'integration, synthesis, cosmogony, faith'. His past he rejected as 'fragmentation, experimentation, scepticism'. With it all came an increased belief in the Catholic hierarchy and monarchy. Not surprisingly, therefore, we find him seeking the Pope's approval of one of his paintings. His hope for the future was clearly stated: 'a religious renaissance based on a progressive form of Catholicism'. Despite such views, and there are many on the subject, he believed he was the only true Surrealist. By such mental gymnastics did he seek to integrate Surrealism into the very aesthetic continuum which it has always set out to destroy.

During those war years in America, his flair for showmanship and publicity stunts, always good for newspaper headlines, made him a

[1]Caresse Crosby's autobiography, *The Passionate Years* (Dial Press, New York, 1953), gives a vivid account of this period.

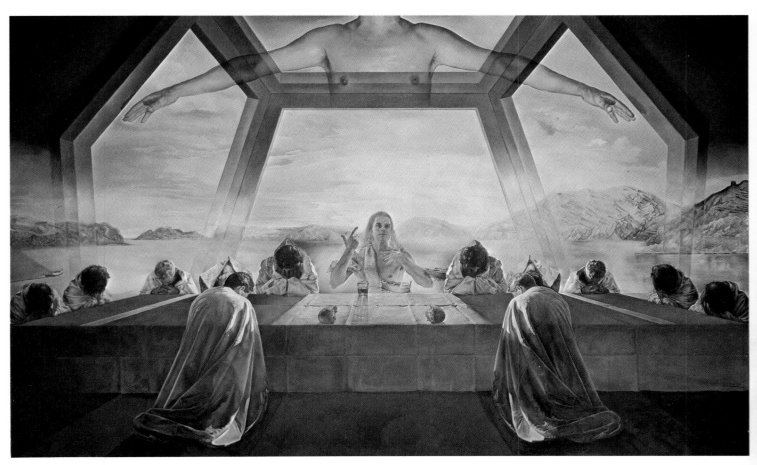

Plate 54 **The Sacrament of the Last Supper**

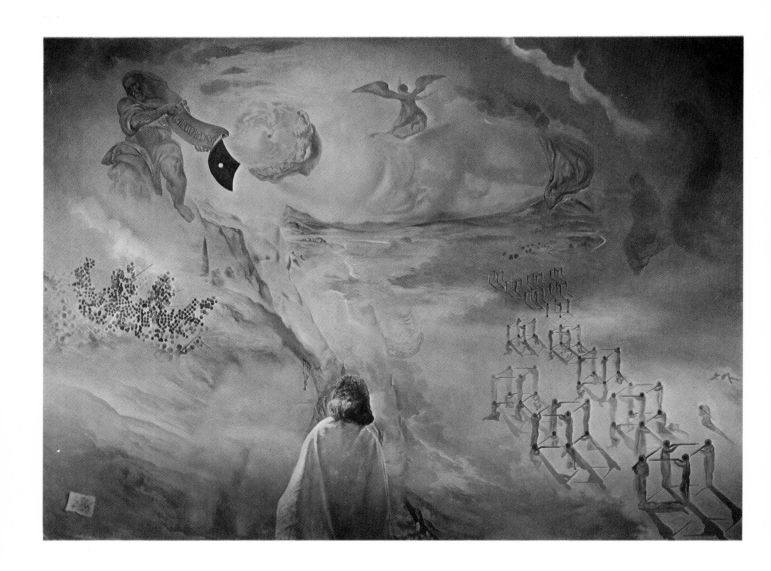

Plate 55
Galacidalacidesoxyribonu-cleicacid
1963
Oil on canvas
122 × 164 in (310.5 × 416.5 cm)
New England Merchants National Bank, Boston (Massachusetts)

The molecular structures that were to appear in a number of works of this period are in this case those of deoxyribonucleic acid.

[1] *The Case of Salvador Dali.*

household name to millions, who confused his money-making clowning with Surrealism. It has accounted for his refusal to separate painting from many minor arts and other aspects of aesthetics. During the early 1940s he painted many portraits of the rich and famous, and it was probably his long association with Jack Warner, the Hollywood producer, in the five years it took to complete his portrait that led to Dali's revived interest in the film as a medium of expression. Hitchcock's *Spellbound* and *The House of Mr Edwards* both had dream sequences by Dali. Not yet realised is his own *The Wheelbarrow of Flesh*, quoted by Fleur Cowles,[1] in which a paranoic woman falls in love with a wheelbarrow. It contains such scenes as swans stuffed with explosives blowing up, rhinoceroses climbing into the Trevi fountain, hundreds of priests on bicycles carrying posters of Malenkov, and a shaven-headed woman, balancing an omelette on her head, standing in the middle of a lake. He has written the book, designed scenery and costumes for two ballets, designed jewellery in collaboration with the Duke di Verdura, and, next to paintings, has devoted considerable time to writing well over thirty books. His widespread activity has also touched on advertising, creating fashions for Chanel and Schiaparelli, and lecture tours to many cities in the United States.

In the meantime, the Surrealists in New York were establishing their presence. Under the editorship of Charles Henri Ford, the bulletin *View* devoted a number of issues to Surrealism, one of which included an attack on Dali by Nicholas Calas called 'I say his flies are ersatz'.[1] In 1942 they started their own review, *VVV*, and the influence was beginning to have an effect on the intellectual life in the States. Dali was to remain isolated from the group's activity, who now referred to him as 'Avida Dollars' ('greedy dollars'), an anagram coined by Breton, or chose only to reproduce one of his advertisements made for Schiaparelli stockings. Unperturbed, Dali continued his own career as a 'completely deviant Surrealist' and set about cornering the religious market. The galactic forms revealed in the whorls of cauliflowers and the nuclear mysticism in the spiral of the rhinoceros horn were now given significance in his new works. In 1947 the Loew-Lewin film company organised a competition for a painting of *The Temptation of St Anthony* to be used in their film *The Private Affairs of Bel Ami*. From the eleven works submitted, five of which were by Surrealists, the jury chose the Max Ernst. Dali's contribution, which was less conventional, was quite the most

Plate 56
Divine Figures in the Wild Landscape of Cape Creus
1970
Oil on copper
Private collection.

[1]'Anti-Surrealist Dali', *View* No. 6, New York, 1941.

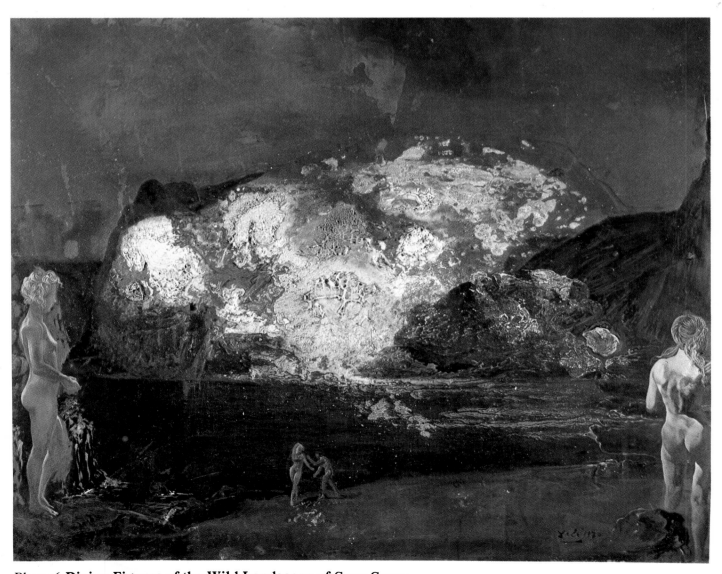

Plate 56 **Divine Figures of the Wild Landscape of Cape Creus**

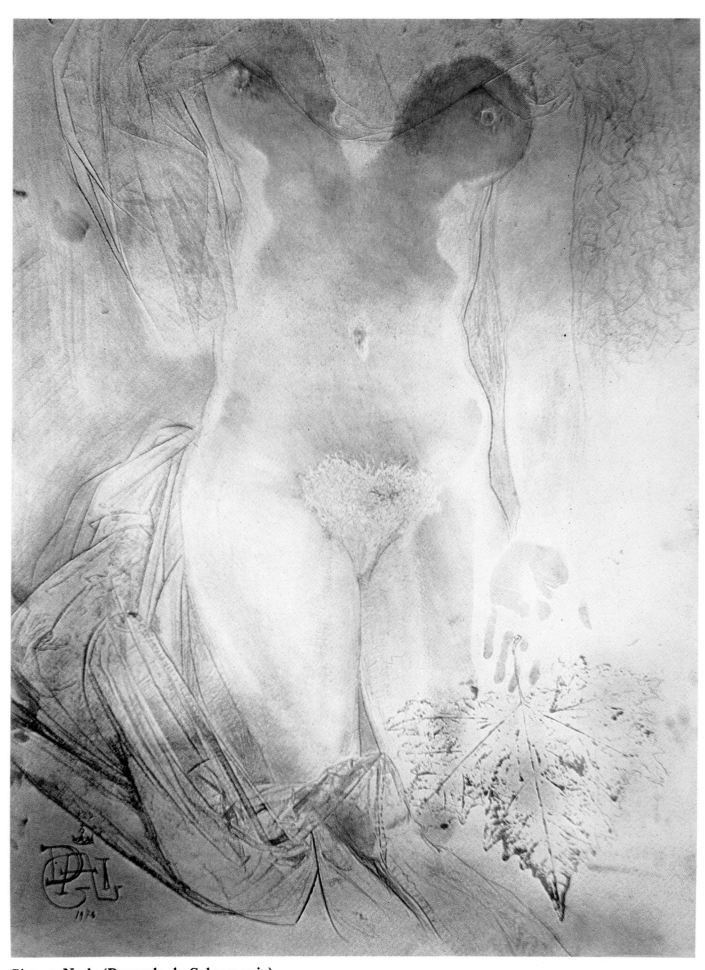

Plate 57 **Nude (Desnudo de Calcomania)**

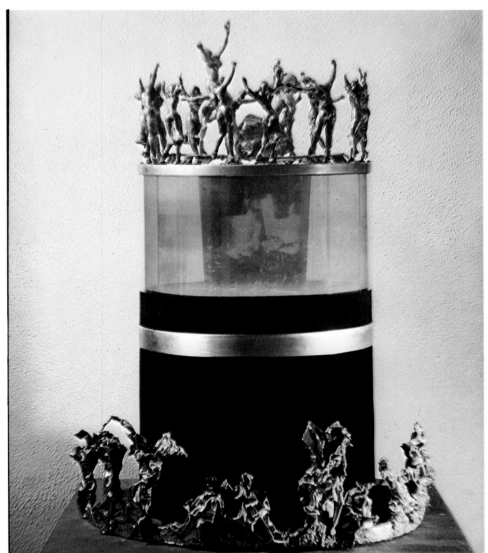

Plate 57
Nude (Desnudo de Calcomania)
1970
Various elements on card
Private collection
Never previously published.

Plate 58
The Shepherd and the Siren
1974
Hologram
Collection Enrique Sabater

outstanding. He wrote about it: 'the hermit sees in the clouds the paranoiac hallucinations of his temptation. The elephants carry on their backs erotic fountains, obelisks, churches, escurials. Elephants stride on almost invisible legs of spiders of desire. With outstretched arm, the saint bears his cross to exorcise the vision.' More revealing are the complex feelings that the picture betrays when one considers how ineffectual the cross appears to be against the advancing horde.

It is during Dali's Classical period that we find him fluctuating both in purpose and in style. The liaison between Freud and Roman Catholicism proposed a new reality, dependent in part on a laborious reconstruction of the past and the incongruities communicated from the subconscious. At the same time, conspicuous technical changes were to become noticeable in Dali's art, characterised by a more romantic handling of colour and a softening of forms that previously had been sharply defined. Also it was abundantly clear that he had no intention of relinquishing his personal symbols, which too often make their appearance in quite unlikely works. These early images once had significance but now become something of a mannerism.

Plate 59
Baisantje Empordanes
1978
Oil on copper
Collection Enrique Sabater

Dali's long interest in the Mannerist and Baroque traditions is noticeable in this painting, with its love of impasto and frenzied brushwork.

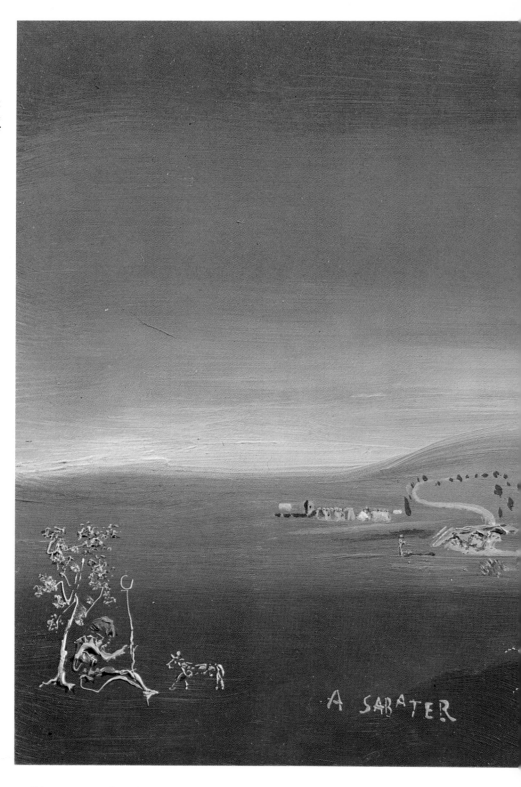

Since 1950 Dali has continued to extend his new mysticism, which was to pass through a number of phases and cover a variety of influences. His mental and plastic resources were brought to bear on the automatism of Abstract Expressionism, and he experimented with shooting lead bullets filled with ink at a lithographic stone for his illustrations to *Don Quixote*. Molecular structures give a new spatial dimension to paintings like *Tuna Fishing*, *The Ascension of St Cecilia* and *Galacidalacidesoxyribonucleicacid* (plate 55). At the same time, he launched as 'the saviour of modern painting' the concept of

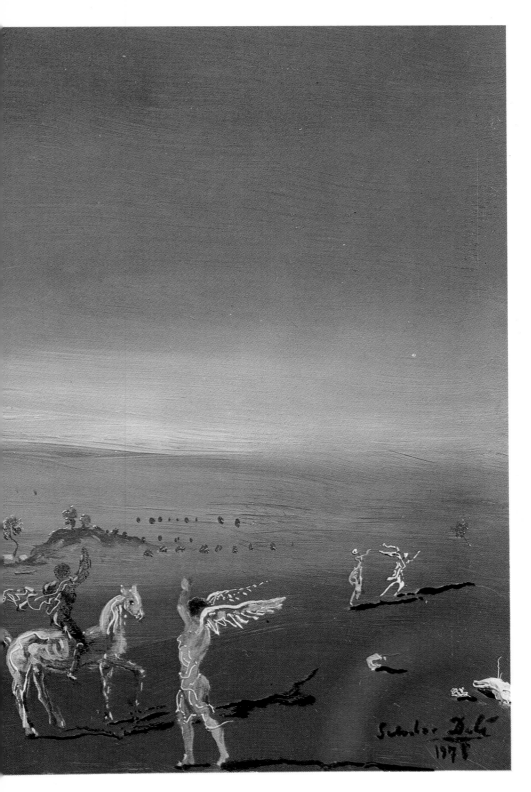

a cosmic Dali,[1] painting rationally his re-found reality.

For half the year, Dali now retires to his beloved Port Lligat in Spain, where he lives like an ascetic, drawing strength from the isolation and peace of the surroundings. For, as he assures us, 'it is difficult to hold the world's interest for more than half an hour at a time. I myself have done so successfully every day for twenty years.' But that was written in 1958, and there is little evidence to suggest that the 'outboard motor continually running', as Picasso described him, is running out of energy.

[1]*Dali by Dali,* Harry N. Abrams Inc., New York, 1970.

chronology

1904   Born 11th May in Figueras, Gerona, Catalonia, Spain.

1914–18   Educated at the Academy of the Brothers of the Marist Order of Figueras.

1918–19   Experimented with Impressionism under the influence of Ramón Pitchot.

1920   Influenced by the Italian Futurists after seeing catalogues and manifestoes brought by his parents from Paris.

1921   Became a pupil at the School of Painting, Sculpture and Drawing in Madrid. Met Luis Buñuel, García Lorca and Pedro Garfias. Discovered Cubism through Juan Gris.

1922   Exhibited paintings at the Dalmau Gallery, Barcelona, with other students' work.

1923   Rejected Cubism and adopted the tenets of the 'Metaphysical School' of paintings which, under the guidance of Giorgio de Chirico and Carlo Carrà, explored the world of inner perception and experience. Suspended for a year from the School for rebellion.

1924   Imprisoned in Gerona for supposed political activity. Illustrated *Les Bruixes de Llers* by Fages de Climent.

1925   Returned to the School in Madrid. First one-man exhibition, Dalmau Gallery, Barcelona. Permanent expulsion from School.

1926–27   Contributed to *Gaseta de les Arts*, Barcelona. Received considerable praise from local art critics. Second one-man show at Dalmau Gallery. Influenced by Cubism and Picasso. Contributed to the journal *L'amic des Arts*.

1927   First visit to Paris. Met Picasso. Painted *Apparatus and Hand* (plate 5).

1927   Second visit to Paris. Miró introduced him to André Breton, Paul Eluard and other Surrealists. Painted *Anna Maria* and *Seated Girl*, shown in Barcelona. Later they were exhibited at the Carnegie Institute in Pittsburg. The first Dali paintings to be shown in America.

1928   Breton, Gala, Paul Eluard and Magritte visited Dali at Cadaqués. His painting now influenced by Ernst and Miró. Produced a group of mixed-media collages.

1929	Painted *Illumined Pleasures* (plate 9), *The Lugubrious Game* (plate 6) and other truly Surrealist works. Joined the Surrealist Group in Paris. First showing of the film *Un Chien Andalou* for which Dali and Buñuel wrote the scenario. In October married Gala.
1929–30	Came under the influence of Art Nouveau and the architecture of Gaudí. Rediscovered de Chirico of the early period (plate 19) as well as the 16th-century fantasies of Arcimboldo (plate 41). Wrote and illustrated *The Visible Woman*, which explained his 'paranoiac-critical method'. Illustrated *The Immaculate Conception* by André Breton and Paul Eluard. Collaborated with Buñuel on the film *The Golden Age* (plate 12), shown in the same year at Studio 28, Paris. In the ensuing riots paintings by Ernst, Miró, Dali, Tanguy and Man Ray were destroyed.
1930–33	Many contributions to the periodical *Surrealism in the Service of the Revolution*. Applied his paranoiac method to the legend of William Tell (plate 23), and the use of the double image in many paintings. Fascinated by Vermeer's *The Artist in his Studio*.
1930–38	Illustrated the second manifesto of Surrealism, *Le Revolver à Cheveux Blancs* by Breton, *Grains et Issues* by Tristan Tzara, *Cours Natural* by Paul Eluard, *Les Chants de Maldoror* by Isadore Ducasse (Comte de Lautréamont). Published an album of six photographs of paintings.
1931–32	Paintings and drawings included in 'The Newer Super-Realism' exhibition at the Wadsworth Atheneum, Hartford, Connecticut. Wrote *L'Amour et la Memoire* and *Babaouo* which included an essay on William Tell and a critique on the cinema. Exhibited at Julien Levy Gallery, New York.
1933	First one-man show, Julien Levy Gallery. Wrote on Millet's *Angelus* in *Minotaure*.
1934	First one-man show in London (Zwemmer Gallery). The Surrealists growing more concerned about his political expressions. Praise of Hitler and monarchist leanings led to official reprimand from Group; no longer attended the Surrealists' meetings. First visit to America. Illustrations of New York in the *American Weekly*.
1934–37	Series of paintings influenced by the effect of light on the beach at Rosas. Hitler, Lenin, *The Angelus* and telephones influence his iconography.
1935	Wrote *The Conquest of the Irrational*, defining his 'paranoiac-critical activity', and attacking abstract art.
1936	Exhibited in the International Surrealist Exhibition in London. Friendship with the English collector, Edward James, who formed the most representative collection of Dali's early work.

1937	Wrote *The Metamorphosis of Narcissus* illustrating his double-image painting of the same name (plate 36). First of three visits to Italy. Influenced by Palladio as well as Renaissance and Baroque paintings.
1938	Through Stefan Zweig and Edward James met Sigmund Freud in London. Made a portrait of him on blotting paper.
1939	Created a Surrealist window for Bonwit-Teller in New York. Arrested for smashing the window. Created 'The Dream of Venus' side show for the New York World's Fair. Published *Declaration of the Independence of the Imagination and of the Rights of Man to his own Madness.* Presentation of his ballet *Bacchanale*, with scenario and scenery by Dali.
1940	Left France for Spain at the beginning of the war. Moved to the United States where he remained until 1948. Lived in California.
1941–42	Major retrospective exhibition, Museum of Modern Art. Shown in eight cities. Established his reputation in the U.S.A. Created sets for the ballets *Labyrinth*, *El Cafe de Chinitas* and *Sentimental Colloquy*. Wrote his autobiography *The Secret Life of Salvador Dali* (Dial Press, New York). Began to paint portraits.
1943	Exhibition at Knoedler Gallery, New York. Completed studies for murals for the home of Helena Rubinstein. Wrote his novel *Hidden Faces* (Dial Press). Illustrations for *The Maze* by Maurice Sandoz; *Essays of Michel de Montaigne*, *As you like it* and *The Autobiography of Benvenuto Cellini*.
1948	Returned to Port Lligat, Spain. Became Classical. Illustrated *50 Secrets of Magic Craftsmanship*.
1949	Made his first religious paintings. *The Madonna of Port Lligat* (plate 50) was sanctioned by the Pope.
1951–52	Illustrations for Dante's *Divine Comedy*. Lectures on 'nuclear mystical' art. Painted *Christ of St John of the Cross* (plate 51). Wrote *Manifesto Mystique* which attempts to explain his mysticism.
1954–55	Published *Dali's Moustache* with Philippe Halsman. Retrospective in Rome. Painted *Corpus Hypercubicus* and *The Last Supper* (plate 54).
1956–59	Dali retrospective at Knokke Le Zoute, Belgium. Wrote *The Cuckolds of Modern Art*. Painted *Santiago El Grande*, now in Beaverbrook Art Gallery, Canada. First historical painting *The Discovery of America*. Wrote *Dali on Modern Art* (Dial Press, New York).
1957	Designed a night club in Acapulco which would move and breathe; the project was never realised.
1958	Married Gala in a religious ceremony in Spain. Lectured at the Theatre de l'Etoile with a 12-metre loaf of bread.
1960	The Surrealists protest at his participation in the Surrealist Exhibition at the d'Arcy Galleries, New York.

1961–63 New edition of *The Secret Life of Salvador Dali. Ballet de Gala* and Scarlatti's opera, *The Spanish Lady and the Roman Cavalier*, with sets and costumes by Dali. Religious painting *The Ecumenical Council* completed, also *The Battle of Tetuan* and *Galacidalacidesoxyribonucleicacid* (plate 55, 1963). Published *The Tragic Myth of the 'Angelus' of Millet* (Jean-Jacques Pauvert, Editeur, Paris).

1964 Awarded one of the highest decorations in Spain, the Grand Cross of Isabella the Catholic.

1964–65 Major exhibition in Tokyo. Wrote *Journal of a Genius*, published in Paris (abridged edition, 1965, Doubleday, New York). Illustrations for the Bible. Began producing 'three-dimensional art' and the *Bust of Dante* sculpture.

1966–73 Alain Bosquet's *Conversations with Dali* (Editions Pierre Belfond. English translation, 1969, E. P. Dutton & Co. Inc., New York). Illustrated a de-luxe edition of *Alice in Wonderland* published by Random House, 1969. Harry N. Abrams Inc., New York, publish *Dali by Dali* with illustrations chosen by the artist and grouped under separate headings – the planetarian, the molecular, the monarchical, the hallucinogenic and the futuristic Dali.

1973 The Dali Museum opened at his birthplace Figueras.

1974 Completed the hologram *The Shepherd and the Siren* for Enrique Sabater. It includes a rare portrait of Gala.

1976 *The Unspeakable Confessions of Salvador Dali* published.

1978 First public showing, in the Teatro Museo Dali in Figueras, of *Babaouo*, a film based on the book first written in 1932.

1979 Retrospective exhibition at the Pompidou Centre, Paris, with a unique installation *La Kermesse Heroique*.

1980 Retrospective exhibition at the Tate Gallery, London.

1982 Created Marquis of Pubol. Gala dies.

bibliography

Barr, Alfred H. Jr, (editor) and Georges Hugnet, *Fantastic Art, Dada, Surrealism*, Museum of Modern Art, New York, 1937

Bosquet, Alain, *Conversations with Dali*, E. P. Dutton & Co. Inc., New York, 1969

Breton, André, *What is Surrealism?*, Faber & Faber, London, 1936. Includes the Introduction to the catalogue of Dali exhibition, Galerie Goemans, Paris, 1929.

Calas, Nicholas, 'Anti-Surrealist Dali: I say his flies are ersatz', *View*, New York, 1941

Cardinal, Roger, and Robert Stuart Short, *Surrealism, Permanent Revelation*, Dutton Pictureback, Studio Vista, London, 1970

Cowles, Fleur, *The Case of Salvador Dali*, Heinemann, London, 1959

Dali by Dali, Abrams, New York, 1970

Dauriac, J. P. *Les Diners de Gala*, Graphis 30. No. 172–152–9. 1974–75

Descharnes, R., *World of Salvador Dali*, Macmillan, 1972

Gascoyne, David, *A Short Survey of Surrealism*, Cobden-Sanderson, London, 1936

Gaunt, William, *Art's Nightmare : the Surrealist Paintings of Salvador Dali*, Studio, London, 1939

Dali, Salvador, *Diary of a Genius*, Hutchinson and New York, 1966

Gerard, Max, *Dali*, London and New York, 1968

Gerard, Max, *Dali-Dali-Dali*, Abrams, New York, 1974

Jean, Marcel, with the collaboration of Arpad Mezei, *The History of Surrealist Painting*, English translation by Simon Watson Taylor, Weidenfeld & Nicolson, London, 1960

Longstreet, Stephen (editor), *Drawings of Dali*, Borden, Los Angeles, 1964

Matthews, J. H., *An Introduction to Surrealism*, Pennsylvania State University Press, 1965

Morse, A. Reynolds, *Salvador Dali 1910–1965*, New York Graphic, 1965

Parrinaud, André, *Unspeakable Confessions of Salvador Dali*, W. H. Allen, 1976

Pierre, José, *Surrealism*, translated from the French by Paul Eve, Heron Books, London, 1970

Read, Herbert (editor), *Surrealism*, Faber & Faber, London, 1936 (paperback edition 1971)

Rubin, William, S., *Dada, Surrealism and Their Heritage*, Museum of Modern Art, New York, 1968

Salvador Dali, exhibition catalogue, Julien Levy Gallery, New York, 1941

Soby, James Thrall, *After Picasso*, Dodd Mead, New York, 1935

Soby, James Thrall, *Salvador Dali*, Museum of Modern Art, New York, 1941

Waldberg, Patrick, *Surrealism*, Thames & Hudson, London, 1965

Waldberg, Patrick, *The Initiators of Surrealism*, Collins in association with UNESCO, London, 1970

acknowledgments

The photographs in this publication were supplied by the owners of the paintings with the following exceptions:

Harry Abrams Inc., New York page 16 top; Joachim Blauel, Munich page 74; British Film Institue, London page 21; Camera Press Ltd, London – Robert Whitaker endpapers, title page right; A. C. Cooper Ltd, London (photographers of the Salvador Dali paintings:– the Edward James & New Trebizond Foundations); DASA Edicones SA, Barcelona back jacket, title page left, 10, 42, 85, 86, 87, 88–9; Roger Jean St Galat, Paris page 68; Photographie Giraudon, Paris page 22; Hamlyn Group Picture Library, London page 58; Hanz Hinz, Basle page 7; Lerner Photography Inc., New York (photographers of the Salvador Dali paintings:– The Mrs & Mrs Reynolds Morse Collection, Salvador Dali Museum, Cleveland, Ohio, and those paintings on pages 11, 12, 19, 30 and 43); Photo Meyer, Vienna page 62.

index

The figures in italic type refer to the captions to the plates.